MAY SKY

MAY SKY

There Is Always Tomorrow

*An Anthology of Japanese American
Concentration Camp Kaiko Haiku*

*Compiled, Translated, and Prefaced
by Violet Kazue de Cristoforo*

SUN & MOON PRESS
LOS ANGELES • 1997

Sun & Moon Press
A Program of The Contemporary Arts Educational Project, Inc.
a nonprofit corporation
6026 Wilshire Boulevard, Los Angeles, California 90036
website: http://www.sunmoon.com

First edition 1997
10 9 8 7 6 5 4 3 2 1

This book was made possible, in part, through a matching grant from
The National Endowment for the Arts, through a matching grant from
The California Arts Council, and through contributions to
The Contemporary Arts Educational Project, Inc., a nonprofit corporation

NATIONAL
ENDOWMENT
FOR ♥ THE
ARTS

Cover: Yasuo Kuniyoshi, *Look It Flies!* (1946)
Reproduced by permission of the Hirshhorn Museum
Design: Katie Messborn
Typography: Guy Bennett

LIBRARY OF CONGRESS CATALOGING IN PUBLICATION DATA
de Cristoforo, Violet Kazue
May Sky: There Is Always Tomorrow
An Anthology of Japanese-American
Concentration Camp Haiku
p. cm
ISBN: 1-55713-253-4
I. Title. II. Author. III. Translator
811'.54—dc20

Printed in the United States of America on acid-free paper.

*In memory of my beloved grandson Sean, 1972—1990,
whose moral support inspired me to complete this anthology,
which I humbly dedicate to the Japanese American Haiku writers
interned during World War II.*

Table of Contents

Foreword

The internment of Japanese Americans during World War II has attracted nationwide attention in recent years. In an effort to reconstruct this very sad event of modern American history, old photographs, sketches, diaries, poems, and newspaper articles have been dug out from attics and closets which record the relocation experience. This anthology compiled by Mrs. de Cristoforo is a unique addition to the growing archive of material testifying to that event. It is a collection of free-style haiku written by the internees, each vividly recreating brief but intense moments during their confinement to the relocation camps. In my opinion, there is no better book to commemorate the 50th anniversary of this authorized relocation of Japanese Americans—Executive Order 9066.

Haiku is a traditional Japanese verse form, normally with a 5-7-5 syllable pattern. In the early 20th century, however, some radical poets in Japan started a free-style movement, advancing the theory that poetic expression should not be restricted by an arbitrary rule like syllable count. This freer form of haiku seems to have had a special appeal to early Japanese settlers in the United States, probably because many of them were, in one sense or another, seekers of freedom in a new land. As Mrs. de Cristoforo describes in this book, the Isseis— first-generation Japanese—formed several free-style haiku clubs at an early stage of their settlement and continued their verse-writing activities even after they were relocated. All of the authors represented in this anthology are amateur poets. They wrote haiku not for poetic fame, but for emotional relief—relief from harsh realities facing them during the war years.

Therein lies the answer to those who may wonder how haiku, often considered nature poetry that sings mainly of flowers and birds, could become a vehicle for presenting painful realities of human life, such as those at war-time relocation camps. Haiku is short in length, but it speaks through its silence, through what it does not expressly state. Haiku poets feel they have vented much emotion and, indeed, they have. For that reason, readers of haiku have to be more active than those of ordinary English poetry, as they are forced to fill in the blanks and capture the emotion not spelled out in words. As one leader of the free-style haiku movement has said, "haiku is only one-half of a circle; it invites each reader to join the poet and complete the other half." In that sense, this anthology offers a rare opportunity for today's readers to share the emotional experience of the war-time internees in a way no other medium of communication can. I hope many readers will take advantage of this opportunity.

Makoto Ueda
Chairman, Asian Studies Department
Professor of Japanese and Comparative Literature
Stanford University

Introduction

This compilation is a diary of the genuine sentiments of the Japanese in America who were evacuated from their homes by the government of the United States and forced to live in internment camps during the Second World War. It is a comprehensive selection of haiku poems symbolizing the ordeal and uncertain future faced by those individuals who were scattered to various detention centers.

It is truly gratifying and meaningful that those poems are available for the first time to a wider readership today, more than 50 years after the War's end. Violet de Cristoforo, who during the War wrote as Kazue Matsuda, has put her heart and soul into this project, overcoming numerous obstacles. My deepest respect is extended to her for publishing this anthology.

For those unfamiliar with contemporary poetry, it should be noted that Kaiko Haiku, the modernist style of haiku—which is not restricted by seasonal words or the 5-7-5 syllable structure of traditional haiku—was initially advocated by my father, Ippekiro Nakatsuka. He founded the Kaiko free-style haiku, as well as the *Kaiko* magazine, long before the Pacific War.

In the early *Taisho* period,* free-style haiku was adopted by

---

* Taisho Era: 1912–1926.

practitioners among the Japanese in America who had emi-grated from Japan. They lived in an environment where sea-sonal changes are not as pronounced as in their native land. The Valley Ginsha, a poetry club in Fresno founded by Neiji Ozawa, and the Delta Ginsha in Stockton, established by Kyotaro Komuro, actively promoted haiku composition among the immigrant community.

When I was invited by the editor to assist in the selection of poems for this anthology, I read through a large collection of haiku written in the various internment camps. I was truly impressed by the fact that the detainees had worked so assidu-ously to weave into their poetry a glimpse of their daily exist-ence—the transition of time in miserable conditions. I under-went a profound emotional experience in reading what came out of this uninspiring environment. So many of the poems contain such rare poetic sensitiveness that I had difficulty in settling on those for inclusion in this volume.

As might be expected, much of the haiku expresses the *Gaman** of the detainees and I felt greatly reassured that their poetry must have been an irreplaceable comfort in such a difficult period and, at the same time, must have provided them intellectual and spiritual sustenance.

I hope the reader will recognize the sentiments of these aged writers, as well as recognize the value of their poetry, especially on this 29th anniversary of the death of Neiji Ozawa—the moving force behind the spread of free-style haiku in America. Noteworthy, also, is that his youngest disciple,

---

* Patience, forbearance, ability to endure.

the American-born and educated Nisei, Kazue Matsuda (presently de Cristoforo) would publish an anthology of Delta and Valley Ginsha poetry to honor the memory of Ozawa and to fulfill his cherished dream of preserving the internees' wartime haiku—something he had not been able to do himself.

The cycle of war and peace may be the fate of mankind. But, looking back, both love and hate have receded into the past and we live today wishing for peace. This haiku anthology is a lesson in peacemaking because, by reminding the present-day generation of the earnest appeals of these victims of war, a greater hope for peace will be born.

Mayumi Nakatsuka

Preface

During my childhood in Hawaii, I became fascinated by the Chinese poetry of Li Po (李白), the Japanese poetry of Shiki Masaoka (正岡子規), and others. My interest in poetry continued to grow and even before World War II, I had joined the Valley Ginsha Haiku Kai (club) and was writing Kaiko (free-style) haiku whenever I had the opportunity.

The modern, free-style haiku was developed by the Tokyo poets Ippekiro Nakatsuka and Kawahigashi Hekigodo in 1915. For these masters, the substance of haiku is that it reduces a thought-picture to its most beautiful essence with a minimum number of words which seem to flow "from heart to heart."

Two of the California free-verse haiku kais (poetry clubs), the Delta Ginsha of Stockton and the Valley Ginsha of Fresno, owe their existence to the aesthetic and intellectual leadership of the pioneering poets Neiji Ozawa and Kyotaro Komuro. The Delta Ginsha was founded in 1918 by Neiji Ozawa and when he moved to Fresno, it continued under the leadership of Kyotaro Komuro. Ozawa organized a second haiku club, the Valley Ginsha, which held its first meeting in 1928.

With the outbreak of the War in 1941, members of the Valley Ginsha were sent to the Fresno Assembly Center, then later most were sent to the Jerome concentration camp in the swampland of Arkansas. After the closing of Jerome, some of its internees were moved to the Rohwer concentration camp (also in Arkansas) and some to the Tule Lake Segregation Cen-

15

ter in Northern California. The Delta Ginsha poets were interned in the Stockton Assembly Center and, subsequently, in the Rohwer concentration camp. In addition, a number of detainees from both haiku societies were sent to the Gila concentration camp in Arizona or to the Justice Department camps at either Santa Fe or Lordsburg, New Mexico, or elsewhere.

During the course of the internment, the Delta Ginsha Haiku Kai, encouraged by its teacher Kyotaro Komuro, had two volumes of its members' haiku published by the *Rohwa Jiho Sha,* the Rohwer Concentration Camp newspaper. The Valley Ginsha, now leaderless because of Neiji Ozawa's diagnosis of tuberculosis and subsequent transfer to the sanatorium at the Gila Indian Reservation, had only a limited number of poems published by the *Utah Nippo,* the Japanese language newspaper of Salt Lake City.

The wartime dispersal resulted in the loss of much of the detainees' haiku, as the belongings they could take with them from camp to camp were usually limited to only the essentials. Ozawa must have had a premonition of this prior to the evacuation. In 1941, as war seemed imminent, he emphasized at one of the last meetings of the Valley Ginsha his concern for the outlook of haiku in America; he stressed that members should try to preserve for future historians their wartime experiences. He also stressed the dilemma that I and others faced—that of being American citizens, yet considered untrustworthy by our own government.

However, one beneficial aspect of this scattering was the variety and power of the haiku the internees wrote. It conveys the emotional impact of being uprooted, and constitutes a poetry of resistance to the inhumanity of war. Further, their haiku reflects the turmoil and anguish they suffered; it is in a class of its own and has made a unique contribution to the field of wartime literature. It is also an important supplement to the history of the internment. Surely, such haiku deserves to be recorded and preserved!

In 1988, Masato (Masando) Ozawa, the adopted son of Neiji Ozawa, our former haiku leader, published a collection of his father's poems entitled *Byoshu*. Some of that haiku has been included in this anthology.

In that same year, I published privately, in *Ino Hana: Poetic Reflections of the Tule Lake Internment Camp—1944*, the few remaining haiku in my possession of the many I had written during the internment, and which had originally been published by the *Utah Nippo*. Now, they are being published in several school textbooks in America.

Then, with encouragement from several haiku authorities both in America and Japan, I resolved to translate the poetry assembled in this anthology—I feel it is the legacy of wartime poets to future generations. Unfortunately, though, many of the verses have already been lost or discarded by these poets' descendants who, unable to read Japanese, did not appreciate the merit of this priceless literary heritage; it might have otherwise totally disappeared if someone had not acted at once.

I was convinced to undertake this onerous and demanding task because I, too, had experienced the same vicissitudes and tribulations as other haiku poets and had written a number of haiku (included in this collection) to give vent to my feelings while being detained in the concentration camps. Had I not compiled this anthology, there is no one left who could have recorded the thoughts and emotions of the former internees.

The poetry selected for inclusion in this collection is an attempt to portray the individuality of each writer and the atmosphere of the various detention centers, each with its own distinctive features. I have narrowed the selection of poems down from several thousand to approximately 300, while retaining as much of the line and image as possible. At the same time, I have striven to remain faithful to the original wording and syntax, letting each poem explain itself.

A translation of poetry, especially haiku, can only at best reproduce the effect that the original poetry had on the translator. For that reason, the poems in this anthology are in Nihongo (Japanese), Romaji or Hepburn System (Japanese written in the Latin alphabet), as well as in the English translation.

Occasionally, it has also been necessary to utilize the Japanese version of the word as well as the English spellings of such expressions as Castle Rock Mountain, mess hall, barracks, camps, and so on. The haiku is also interesting for the inventiveness displayed by the internees in creating new words for such places as Rohwer (朗和), Tule Lake (鶴嶺湖), Denson (電遜), and Denver (伝馬).

In this collection, all translations from English to Japanese and vice versa, are not literal, but are free renditions of the originals.

I am confident that haiku enthusiasts will be inspired by this poetry to have a better understanding of the anguish and suffering of Japanese Americans detained behind the barbed wire fences of the concentration camps and their ingenious ways of surviving their ordeal. It is also my earnest hope that the anthology will bring solace to the spirits of the former internees who died tragically in the camps, as well as to those who have passed on since, unaware of the United States government's apology for their unjust and illegal removal and detention.

Violet Kazue de Cristoforo
Salinas, California
1996

History of Kaiko Haiku and the Haiku Clubs

The Kaiko style of haiku began in Japan in 1915 when Ippekiro Nakatsuka (1879–1946), its founder, stressed the importance of fulfilling human nature through direct expression of the poet's emotions and giving circumstances enthusiastic attention in order to satisfy the creative drive. Two years later Ippekiro published the first Kaiko magazine.

Kaiko (海紅) means crimson sea. It was named after the crimson-colored flowering quince (*boke*), which grew in abundance around the inn where Nakatsuka lived. His love for the crimson-colored flowers was used to illustrate his intense abstract feeling, and was used for the cover of his monthly haiku magazine to advocate the revolutionary new style haiku.

In the early 1930s, a group of Japanese avant-garde haiku poets who considered the traditional haiku style (such as Hototogisu) suitable primarily for the gentle elderly, established a free-form group using the Kaiko style which allowed them to deviate from the restrictive expressions of scenery and objective subtleness associated with the earlier classical haiku.

These new rising forms of haiku stimulated the emergence of a free, intuitive expression of one's state of mind. Love and observation of nature, vivid and youthful expression of detail and elegant usage of words correlated with the season were to become the focal points. The free-style Kaiko haiku spread quickly among the dissatisfied young poets.

In North America, Neiji Ozawa, who had previously founded the Delta Ginsha Haiku Kai, following his graduation from University of California at Berkeley, also established the Valley Ginsha Haiku Kai in Fresno. Its members met monthly and submitted their haiku to the master of the month, who was usually the host or hostess for the evening. They submitted for consideration as many poems as they desired. The poems were then read and discussed and a vote was taken to determine the best haiku. There were usually 15–20 members at these meetings, and their dues were nominal—just enough to purchase refreshments for the evening.

By the time the meeting convened, the Master would have already copied the haiku, concealing the author's identity, and made enough copies for distribution to each attending member. If necessary, use of more symbolic words, or enhancement of feeling were proposed and agreed upon before final corrections were made. This procedure was followed for each haiku presented.

Finally, votes were cast for the best haiku of the evening and only then would the Master reveal the name of each poet. It was an evening anticipated by the members—grape growers, onion farmers, teachers, housewives, bankers, pharmacists, and others—who had assembled for an enlightening cultural and social event.

At the outbreak of hostilities, fearing reprisals, the majority of Japanese Americans, including Central California haiku poets, destroyed most of their collections, including all forms of Japanese literature. Their forced evacuation and ongoing relocation from camp to camp resulted in many of the poems written during that period never being recovered. Similar losses were suffered by Japanese haiku writers in Japan as a result of the innumerable bombings by the US Army Air Force. In one particularly heavy incendiary raid on Tokyo, the Kaiko depository of haiku books and literary materials was completely lost.

The post-war period saw several former Valley and Delta Ginsha members expatriated or repatriated to Japan. Others scattered throughout the United States, with a handful returning to Central California. These few individuals made a diligent attempt to make a living and restore their lives, in spite of the prejudice and discrimination still extant. The passing of the once energetic free-style Kaiko groups, especially the Delta Ginsha Haiku Kai and the Valley Ginsha Haiku Kai (which had been known for their international flavor and capable women poets), was a tragedy to the ethnic Japanese communities.

Valley Ginsha Haiku Kai Poetry
Written Prior to World War II

Contrary to the general belief that all immigrants from the Far East were from rural areas and uneducated, pre-war Japanese immigrants had the potential to write and express themselves adequately, but most of them were prevented from doing so by the necessity of simply making a living in the hostile and discriminating economic conditions they encountered in America.

The poets' pre-war haiku expresses peacefulness and tranquility, as well as hope for their future in America. As indicated by author Issi Fukushima in his book *Pursuing The Origin of Kaiko*,

> It is said that their gaiety and bright atmosphere brought unusual emotional spirit to the Kaiko…. Having established their own unique life style over the years with their exceptional talent, they were enjoying life…however, their ambitious plans were disrupted with the abrupt war between Japan and the United States, which thrust them into a bottomless pit.★

★ This excerpt is a literal translation of the Japanese original.

In contrast with the poets' pre-war haiku, what was written in the camps reveals the internees' dejection, the oppressiveness of their lives behind barbed wire, and the sadness caused by this tragedy which daily faced them.

This contrast is highlighted by Neiji Ozawa's haiku written while he was in the Gila Indian reservation sanatorium from which the title of this anthology is derived:

> From the window of despair
> May sky
> There is always tomorrow

Like a comet, some of the wartime haiku writers emerged only momentarily from obscurity, flashed across the literary firmament and, when the war ended and the infamous concentration camps closed, vanished into oblivion.

With the exception of myself, all of the poets from both the Delta and Valley Ginsha Haiku Kais are deceased; therefore, very little factual information is available about them. Yet, unknown to the haiku writers, their mark of greatness was left on the literature of the Japanese-American internment, and their haiku is a poignant reminder of their wartime experiences.

On the following pages are some of the haiku written by the Valley Ginsha Haiku Kai members at their last meeting prior to the War. These poems were published December 8, 1941 by the *Shinsekai Asahi Shimbun,* a Japanese-American newspaper in San Francisco, California.

1936. Left to right: Hekisamei Matsuda, son Kenji, and the author, Kazue Matsuda.

Picnicking, 1938. Left to right: Neiji Ozawa, Kazue Matsuda, Hekisamei Matsuda with son Kenji, and Reiko Gyomo.

秋陽こころよし一人ゑんどうをまいてゐる朝　　　雫

花黄色とはつきり見えて来て秋野明ける　　　玲子

たがひに沖に釣る親しさ潮をへだてものいふ　　　正

西陽まだあつしダリア切る僕にとんぼとまり　　　小紅子

32

AKIBI KOKOROYOSHI HITORI ENDO O MAITE IRU ASA

Pleasant autumn sun
I am sowing green peas
alone in the morning

(Shizuku)

HANA KIIRO TO HAKKIRI MIETE KITE AKINO AKERU

The flower is yellow
I see it clearly now
dawn on autumn field

(Reiko)

TAGAI NI OKI NI TSURU SHITASHISA SHIO O HEDATE MONO IUU

Fishing on the ocean
talking to one another
in friendship across the distance

(Sho)

NISHIBI MADA ATUSHI DARIA KIRU BOKU NI TONBO TOMARI

Westering sun still hot
I am cutting dahlias
dragonfly alights on me

(Shokoshi)

33

われら四人の子とゐて秋のそらすみ　　　　　　美篠

秋の日暮るる建坊ケンゲキを覚え　　　　　碧沙明

とめと霜にいたまれ地の赤い実青い実　　　未草

菊も咲き誰彼に声をかけたいお天気続く　一恵

34

WARERA YONIN NO KO TO ITE AKI NO SORA SUMI

We are with four children
clear autumn sky

(Bisho)

AKI NO HI KURURU KEN-BO* KENGEKI O OBOE

Autumn sun setting
Ken-bo learning
sword fighting skills

(Hekisamei)

TOMATO SHIMO NI ITAMARE CHI NO AKAI MI AOI MI

Tomatoes damaged by frost
red and green fruit
on the ground

(Miso)

KIKU MO SAKI TAREKARE NI KOE O KAKETAI OTENKI TSUZUKU

Chrysanthemum also in bloom
continuing fair weather
wish to chat with people

(Kazue)

* Nickname of his son Kenji.

35

国のつわもの菊咲く垣べりを通り　　　　弘

日覆を直すずつと桃黄葉繁みにはしごを入れ　　寧次

36

KUNI NO TSUWAMONO KIKU SAKU KAKIBERI O TOORI

Chrysanthemum blooming
near fence
American soldier passes

(Hiroshi)

HIOI O NAOSU ZUTTO MOMOKIBA SHIGEMINI HASHIGO O IRE

Mending sunshade
placing ladder into
thick yellow leaves of peachtree

(Neiji)

Haiku Leaders: Ozawa and Komuro

To appreciate more fully the poetry which was generated from the two Ginsha Clubs, a closer look at each of its leaders, Neiji Ozawa and Kyotaro Komuro, is in order. Poetry written by each of these leaders which follows them through their relocation from camp to camp gives us further insight into these men.

Ozawa, Neiji (*Valley Ginsha Haiku Club*)

Neiji Ozawa was born on September 28, 1886 in Nagano Prefecture, Japan. He was the third son of a former village mayor who was also a well-to-do tradesman in hemp cloth and, later, an owner of a dry goods business.

When he was about a year old, his mother died and he was given to his uncle and family to be raised. After several years, he returned home and graduated from elementary school. His stay was short-lived, as when his father remarried, he was sent off to Fujimori Academy, an exclusive Juku (private school) for the privileged sons of the local elite. During this period, Ozawa became interested in haiku and joined a circle of haiku poets. His association with them continued even after he moved to Tokyo to work for a pharmaceutical wholesaler.

Ozawa's flair for literary taste and poetic inspiration can be attributed to several factors. His father also wrote haiku and his grandfather was a close associate of Japan's literary scholar and lyric poet Hirotsuna Sasaki—whose son, Nobutsuna Sasaki, was editor-supervisor of the Tanka *Journal Kokoro-No-Hana*. (Tanka is a short Japanese verse of 31 syllables.) Other contributing factors are that Nagano Prefecture, also known as Shinshu, thrived on haiku since ancient times, and the town of Suwa, where Ozawa grew up, was the birthplace of the priest who accompanied Basho, the poetic genius of Haiku (1644–1694). His masterpiece was *Oku-No-Hosomichi* which, translated, means "Narrow Path to Oshu."

At his place of work Neiji Ozawa was known as a strong-willed individual with a unique personality. Such characteristics could have been the result of being raised by his uncle. His step mother and the children born to her, as well as his father's poor health, could have been factors contributing to his desire to go to America. In San Francisco he could also find a distant relative who was a practicing physician.

So, in 1907, he boarded a ship for Seattle. Among the passengers was Kyotaro Komuro, with whom Ozawa eventually formed a life-long friendship. This association in time led to the formation of the haiku movement in America.

About four years later, he enrolled at the University of California at Berkeley to study pharmacology. In spite of the rigors of his studies (which were conducted in English), Ozawa became politically active within the Japanese community. In 1913, he participated in a short-lived, student-led movement to demand naturalization rights for Asians. He also joined the community-wide protests against the passage of the Alien Land Law.

Ozawa graduated from Berkeley in 1915. That same year, he opened a pharmacy in San Francisco, and established the first Kaiko society in the United States. Two years later, he moved to Stockton where, in 1918, he founded the Delta Ginsha Haiku Kai with the assistance of his friend, Kyotaro Komuro, who later became its leader. Four years later, Ozawa moved south to Fresno, where Japanese tenant farmers and laborers were establishing orchards and vineyards.

Pre-war photo of Neiji Ozawa, founder and leader of Valley Ginsha, standing with his wife in front of his Fresno pharmacy on "F" Street.

It was at this time that he married. While living in Fresno, he set up another pharmacy. He was soon looked upon as a medical expert because Japanese doctors were scarce, and white physicians were unacceptable due not only to the language barrier, but the prohibitive costs. Although not a physician, years later Ozawa wrote and published an 800-page medical almanac called *Guide For The Sick Person (Byosha No Gaido)* so that farmers in isolated areas could diagnose their own condition. His experience caring for the ill and dying later surfaced in his poetry describing his own bouts with tuberculosis.

Not long after his arrival in Fresno, Ozawa also organized the Valley Ginsha Haiku Kai. The first meeting of that poetry club, attended by 14 members, was held at his home on Ventura Avenue in 1928. The first combined Delta Ginsha/Valley

Ginsha meeting was held in Stockton on January 5, 1929, attended by 40 members; over 300 haiku were presented for critique.

In 1935, not having any children, Ozawa adopted his sister's fourth son Masato (Masando), who was living in Japan.

In 1942, following his internment in the Fresno Assembly Center, he became ill with tuberculosis and was transferred to the Gila Indian Reservation Sanatorium in south-central Arizona so he could receive treatment. In spite of this unforeseen development, he still managed to correspond with members of both the Valley Ginsha and Delta Ginsha, wherever they were, to give them advice and to critique their work. Much of this corres-pondence remains in the possession of his adopted son, Masato.

At Gila there were no haiku activities, and Ozawa was forced to send some of his haiku to the Tule Lake Valley Ginsha Haiku Kai for inclusion with theirs.* Much of Ozawa's haiku was later sent to his adopted son, Masato, in Japan and, still later, made available for inclusion in this anthology.

After the War, Ozawa and his wife returned to Fresno where they resided until their return to Japan in 1963 because of illness. Neiji Ozawa died in Tokyo on July 22, 1967, at the age of 80.

Much of the biographical data of the members of both the Delta and Valley Ginsha Haiku Kais were lost or destroyed in the turbulent days following the Pearl Harbor attack. For that reason, *Byoshu* and its supplement, the publications of Ozawa's adopted son, had to be relied upon for much of the biographical material in this anthology.

---

* Neiji Ozawa's haiku is listed with that of the Tule Lake Valley Ginsha Group (p. 214).

Photo of pre-war Fresno Valley Ginsha members taken at Roeding Park, Fresno, California, 1928

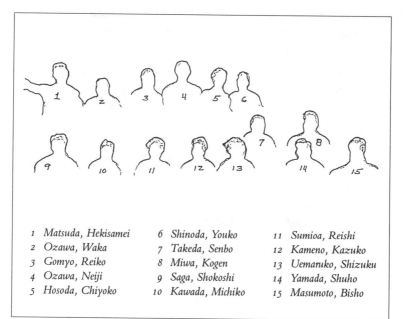

1 Matsuda, Hekisamei	6 Shinoda, Youko	11 Sumioa, Reishi
2 Ozawa, Waka	7 Takeda, Senbo	12 Kameno, Kazuko
3 Gomyo, Reiko	8 Miwa, Kogen	13 Uemaruko, Shizuku
4 Ozawa, Neiji	9 Saga, Shokoshi	14 Yamada, Shuho
5 Hosoda, Chiyoko	10 Kawada, Michiko	15 Masumoto, Bisho

KOMURO, KYOTARO (SHOICHI) (*Delta Ginsha Haiku Club*)

Kyotaro Komuro was born in Shimoda, Izu Peninsula, Shizuoka Prefecture, in 1885. He took the pen name "Kyotaro" from the given name of Izumi Kyoka (泉鏡花), a contemporary poet and literary giant Komuro greatly admired.

Komuro and Neiji Ozawa came to America on the same ship and became close friends. They landed in Seattle, Washington on August 31, 1907 and eventually moved to San Francisco. Ozawa remained there, but Komuro went on to Stockton and became president and publisher of the Stockton Times. In 1917, Ozawa joined him and the following year they established the Delta Ginsha Haiku Kai (club), which took its name from the marshes at the delta of the San Joaquin River.

During Komuro's internment in the Stockton Assembly Center and the Rohwer Concentration Camp, so much creative writing was made possible through his dedication and initiative, which, in turn, inspired the Delta Ginsha poets to express *their* personal perceptions and emotions. This initiated the "golden age" of Delta Ginsha. Through his insight and commitment, Komuro kept his group together and their haiku output has remained the apex of their wartime experiences and tribulations. While at Rohwer, Komuro edited and published Volumes I and II of the Delta Ginsha Haiku Collection.

After the War, Komuro relocated to Denver, Colorado where he managed and operated a printing shop, published the *Colorado Jiji* (a Japanese vernacular newspaper), and formed a Denver Delta Ginsha which met at his home. During this time, his wife operated a grocery store and his two sons attended college. Komuro died in Colorado in 1953 at the age of 68 as a result of a fatal automobile accident while on a fishing trip.

In his eulogy, Ozawa said that Komuro's excellent haiku captures every phase of the internment experience, and expresses the vivid life style of the internees' confused existence. Komuro was Ippekiro Nakatsuka's most loyal and devoted kaiko pupil, and the shining star of Jiruyitsu (freestyle) haiku in North America. For Komuro, haiku was paradise because he saw poetry in every aspect of America's environment and life; he should be lauded as a journalist and as a human being.

Komuro's last haiku, written just before his death, exemplifies his stoic philosophy and humanism:

よく生きて来た七十年道草枯れそむ

YOKU IKITE KITA SHICHIJUNEN MICHI KUSA KARE SOMU

Lived well seventy years
roadside grass
begins to wither

Valley Ginsha/Delta Ginsha Combined Haiku Conference at Kyotaro Komuro's residence, January 5, 1929.

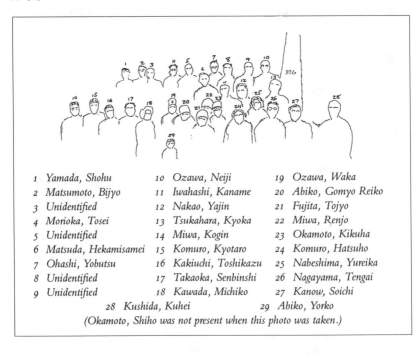

1 Yamada, Shohu	10 Ozawa, Neiji	19 Ozawa, Waka
2 Matsumoto, Bijyo	11 Iwahashi, Kaname	20 Abiko, Gomyo Reiko
3 Unidentified	12 Nakao, Yajin	21 Fujita, Tojyo
4 Morioka, Tosei	13 Tsukahara, Kyoka	22 Miwa, Renjo
5 Unidentified	14 Miwa, Kogin	23 Okamoto, Kikuha
6 Matsuda, Hekamisamei	15 Komuro, Kyotaro	24 Komuro, Hatsuho
7 Ohashi, Yobutsu	16 Kakiuchi, Toshikazu	25 Nabeshima, Yureika
8 Unidentified	17 Takaoka, Senbinshi	26 Nagayama, Tengai
9 Unidentified	18 Kawada, Michiko	27 Kanow, Soichi

28 Kushida, Kuhei   29 Abiko, Yorko

(Okamoto, Shiho was not present when this photo was taken.)

*Uprooting and Relocation
to Concentration Camps*

OUSTER OF ALL JAPANESE ANNOUNCED

Babies, orphans, adopted children, and children of multiple ancestry were ordered incarcerated. The military arbitrarily decided that persons with as little as 1/16 "Japanese blood" were to be detained and incarcerated.

The internment of Japanese Americans living on the West Coast involved a process by which they were registered, numbered, tagged with shipping labels, and placed aboard buses, trains or trucks for shipment, under armed guard, to temporary locations euphemistically called "Assembly Centers."

These centers were located, for the most part, on county fairgrounds and racetracks, in the western part of the United States. The malodorous horse stalls became the internees' living quarters until permanent locations, also euphemistically called "Relocation Centers," were established in the interior of the country. Except for personal belongings the detainees could carry, the only furnishings they were issued consisted of cots, army blankets and straw-filled mattresses.

About a month after President Franklin D. Roosevelt signed Executive Order 9066 authorizing the evacuation of Japanese Americans, the War Relocation Authority ("WRA") was established to facilitate the detainees' internment. By November 1942, the 15 assembly centers and the 10 relocation centers had been transferred from US Army control to the WRA, under whom they remained until 1944. (For the sake of simplicity, "WRA" has been omitted from the names of all detention centers.)

Concentration camps are usually defined as either locations where prisoners of war, enemy aliens and political prisoners are confined or as prison camps where political dissidents and members of minority groups are imprisoned. While the term "concentration camp" was not, in general, publicly used in reference to these confinement centers, literature alluding to the detention of Japanese Americans is replete with just this term. Further, it was a term used often by Presidents Roosevelt and Harry Truman, Attorney General Biddle, the Joint Chiefs of Staff, and various other government officials.

What follows is a description of a few of the assembly centers and concentration camps, as well as Justice Department detention centers. It is within these particular camps that much of the haiku contained in this anthology was written.

Caucasian neighbors bidding Japanese family good-bye.

Family grieving as head of family is arrested by FBI agent.

Another "disloyal"? March 1942

KEY

ASSEMBLY CENTERS*
Puyallup, Wash.
Portland, Ore.
Marysville, Calif.
Sacramento, Calif.
Tanforan, Calif.
Stockton, Calif.
Turlock, Calif.
Merced, Calif.
Pinedale, Calif.
Salinas, Calif.
Fresno, Calif.
Tulare, Calif.
Santa Anita, Calif.
Pomona, Calif.
Mayer, Ariz.

■ **RELOCATION CENTERS***
Manzanar, Calif.
Tule Lake, Calif.
Poston, Ariz.
Gila, Ariz.
Minidoka, Ida.
Heart Mountain, Wyo.
Granada, Colo.
Topaz, Utah
Rohwer, Ark.
Jerome, Ark.

● **JUSTICE DEPARTMENT
INTERNMENT CAMPS**
Santa Fe, N. Mex.
Bismarck, N. Dak.
Crystal City, Tex.
Missoula, Mont.

△ **CITIZEN ISOLATION CAMPS**
Moab, Utah
Leupp, Ariz.

▨ Military Area 2 or
"Free Zone" until March 29, 1942

PLEASE SEE EXPLANATORY COMMENTS ON ℓ
FOLLOWING PAGE

Map of US concentration camps

Assembly Centers

FRESNO ASSEMBLY CENTER

The Central Valley of California, where the City of Fresno is located, has a world-wide reputation for agricultural products, including oranges, grapes, raisins, and wine. In pre-war days, most of the field workers were of Japanese ancestry.

In the spring of 1942, some 5,000 Japanese Americans from the counties of Amador, Madera, Fresno, Kings and Tulare were evacuated from their homes and interned by the US Army in the hastily-constructed and thoroughly inadequate Fresno Assembly Center. This temporary location was composed of infield and outfield areas of the racetrack at the Fresno Fairgrounds. The Japanese Americans living west of Highway 99 (which divides California vertically) were arbitrarily evacuated first. Those living east of the highway were not evacuated until the summer of 1942. This action caused many families to be separated for the first time in their lives, resulting in much emotional stress and illness.

The largest group of detainees came from the Florin area of Amador County, south of Sacramento. They were housed in 80 barracks at the southern end of the racetrack. This tree-lined area, termed the "fig garden area," provided shade from the scorching summer sun. Other detainees were not so fortunate. In the barren areas of the racetrack, some of the more resourceful detainees sought relief from the unrelenting heat—temperatures often soared above 100° F (35°C)—by ripping up the flimsy floorboards of their one-room living quarters, digging a hole, wetting their clothes and crawling into the holes they had dug.

Detainees also resorted to harvesting and eating alfalfa wherever they could find it, including that growing between the ill-fitted floor planks. The internees, who had been accustomed to eating abundant fresh vegetables while living in the rich farmlands of the San Joaquin River and Fresno Valleys, simply did not find palatable the canned Army-supplied vegetables served in the Center's mess halls. Because they avoided eating them whenever possible, the alfalfa they harvested replaced the fresh vegetables they were used to. Alfalfa was made into salads and was also used to make *tsukemono* (pickled vegetables).

At the beginning of detention at the Fresno Assembly Center, many detainees developed symptoms of food poisoning. Improper preparation of food by inexperienced cooks and lack of refrigeration in the stifling summer heat were contributing causes. As well, there were a substantial number of internees who suffered allergy-related illnesses due to the straw which Camp authorities required they use to fill their "ticks" (mattress covers). In both instances, the detainees' symptoms could not be ameliorated, even by visits to the camp hospital. The inability to treat these illnesses was a direct result of the lack of appropriate medicine. The only medication available to the detainees were such items as rubbing alcohol, iodine and aspirin—easily purchased by doctors at neighborhood drug stores.

Fifty years later, this overall lack of concern is difficult to believe. The wretched living conditions and lack of appropriate medicine led to the eventual death of some of the detainees. These atrocities became the subject of several poignant haiku penned by Neiji Ozawa.

The detainees lived at the Fresno Assembly Center until the fall of 1942, when it finally closed. They were then moved to permanent camps located either in the desert (Gila Concentration Camp in Arizona) or other inland wilderness areas (mainly Jerome Concentration Camp, near the town of Lake Village, Arkansas, close to the Mississippi Delta).

Today, California Registered Historical Landmark No. 934 at the entrance of the Fresno County Fairground commemorates the former Fresno Assembly Center.

Henry Sugimoto

"Fig Garden Area"—the only shady location of the Fresno Assembly Center

Internees waiting in scorching sun for their meal at Fresno Assembly Center mess hall.

Wash rooms of Fresno Assembly Center had many uses.

The City of Stockton lies approximately 90 miles east of San Francisco, California and is known for its agricultural products and its port facilities on the San Joaquin River Delta. At the outbreak of the War there were several thousand Japanese Americans living in that area, when the US Army, under order from the President, forcibly evacuated and detained these citizens in the Stockton Assembly Center with only the possessions they could carry.

At the assembly center located on the San Joaquin County Fairgrounds, the 4,271 first and second generation Japanese Americans from the San Joaquin Delta were housed in 196 primitive and hastily-built barracks within the racetrack area from May to December 1942. The housing was so inadequate that some of the internees were even placed in the horse stalls, where the stench of horse urine and manure was unbearable. Memories of the discrimination they suffered, and the outrage at such an existence in the heat of summer, are expressed in many of the haiku written by the Delta Ginsha poets during their five-month confinement in Stockton. These haiku are compiled in Volume 1 of the Delta Ginsha Haiku Collection published in the *Rohwa Jiho Sha* by the poets' haiku teacher, Kyotaro Komuro.

On May 12, 1984, a plaque designating a California Historical Landmark was erected just outside the main gate of the former Assembly Center.

Concentration Camps

One of the most severe endurance tests experienced by the internees was that undergone by the two groups which were moved from the Fresno and Stockton Assembly Centers in California to either the Jerome or Rohwer Concentration Camps in southeastern Arkansas.

Weary from culling the few personal belongings they were allowed to take, from the slow and tiresome administrative processing and from the minutiae imposed by the authorities, the detainees—including those caring for young children or elderly parents and relatives—were put on dilapidated trains in the fall of 1942 for the four-day, five-night trip to their destination.

The overcrowded trains had only primitive, unclean toilets and no eating or sleeping facilities. The passengers, even the young and the aged, were confined to their seats during the extremely tiring trip, except for those rare occasions when the train stopped in uninhabited areas and the detainees were allowed to stretch their legs for a short time, always surrounded by armed and trigger-happy military policemen.

In the early fall of 1942, in spite of the lingering summer heat, the trains were routed south from Fresno to Yuma, Arizona, then east across the most desolate and parched areas to their final destination of Arkansas—all locations subsequently mentioned by many of the internees in their haiku.

In the oppressive heat, with a scarcity of drinking water, no conveniences for preparing baby formula or easing the discomfort of young and old, the long trip was an ordeal for the detainees. To make matters worse, the guards insisted that the window shades be drawn for security reasons, especially when the trains were side-tracked to allow passage of military trains or when travelling through inhabited areas.

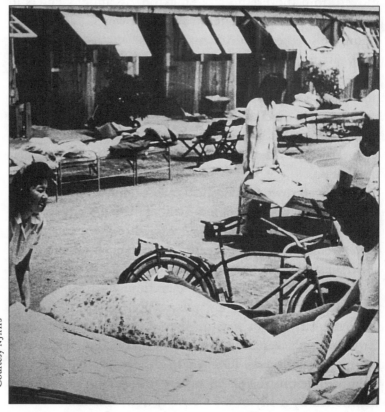

Courtesy NJAHS

INTERNEES AIRING BEDDING

Horsestalls became living quarters until the more permanent camps were established. Each "apartment" was furnished with cots, army blankets, and oftentimes, straw-filled mattresses.

Jerome Concentration Camp was where the majority of internees from the Fresno Assembly Center were first sent. At their Jerome destination, located near Denson, Arkansas not far from the Mississippi Delta, trains were met by army ambulances which transported the ill and the infirm to the camp hospital. However, only minimal care was available because the hospital had not yet been completed and equipment and medicines were in short supply.

Most of the internees had come from the healthier climates of California and, in some cases, balmy Hawaii. Not only had they become depressed by their swampland surroundings, they were often frightened by the ominous black clouds that nearly always preceded the frequent rainstorms and accompanying bolts of lightening, thunder and pounding hail. In the summer, their distress increased because they were tormented by the swarms of mosquitoes, chiggers and ticks which infested the area. In winter, they sank up to their ankles in the mire whenever they were forced to cut the green firewood they had to use for their heating stoves.

The Denson Valley Ginsha, named for the town of Denson, was founded by the Fresno poets now confined in Jerome. They met occasionally and penned some moving haiku about the miserable conditions in which they found themselves. However, with the exception of a few poems written at the "Farewell Haiku Meeting" (included in this anthology), most of the haiku written by the Denson Valley Ginsha was lost in the subsequent moves of its members from one internment camp to another.

The Rohwer Concentration Camp, located in the swampland of Arkansas near the Mississippi Delta, was one of 10 permanent detention centers operated by the WRA. In the fall of 1942, a contingent of Stockton Assembly Center internees, along with a group from the Santa Anita Assembly Center near Los Angeles, were moved to this camp located 70 miles southeast of Little Rock, Arkansas.

As in Jerome, weather conditions were extreme. Average rainfall was 61 inches annually; the area was very cold in the winter; and in the summer, the humidity was about seven times higher than what the internees were accustomed to in California. The detainees not only had to contend with troublesome insects like mosquitoes, chiggers and ticks, but also with some of the most poisonous snakes in America, varieties of which often reached a length of six or seven feet.

The barracks were tar paper covered, hastily-erected structures with ill-fitting doors and windows which did not close properly. As well, there was no running water and no coal supplies for heating stoves.

As one of their first tasks, the internees were forced to cut the dense swampland growth for firewood and to clear the area for growing vegetables for their own use, as well as for growing cotton, soy beans and rice later on. The firewood cut by the detainees, however, was green and usually wet. It was not only difficult to burn, but filled their living quarters with clouds of acrid smoke, blackening everything and making it difficult to breathe. Whenever the internees went out of doors, usually to use the communal facilities, cut firewood, report to their work details or attend meetings, they sank up to their ankles in the ooze of the swamp.

As was also the case in Jerome, many of the male internees volunteered for military service, leaving behind parents, relatives and friends. This caused considerable anxiety and mixed feelings on both sides.

The harsh physical conditions under which the internees had to live, coupled with the emotional stress of losing family members and continuing to be uprooted, gave rise to many unique expressions reflected in the poets' haiku.

By the time this camp closed in November 1945, some 8,475 internees had been detained here. All that remains of the Rohwer Concentration Camp, listed as a Historical Site in 1974, are 24 stone markers over the graves of deceased internees and two memorials to the 31 Nisei soldiers from Rohwer who were killed in the European Theater of Operation.

Henry Sugimoto of Hanford, California, well-known for his many oil paintings and sketches of camp scenes, left an extensive pictorial record of the lives of the internees from the Fresno Assembly Center and the Jerome and Rohwer Concentration Camps. Several paintings are included throughout this anthology.

One of the many boundary signs posted around Tule Lake Segregation Center.

TULE LAKE SEGREGATION CENTER

At the end of 1942, the War Department decided to organize a volunteer combat team of Nisei (second generation Japanese-American) soldiers made up of those who had passed a so-called loyalty review. The WRA saw this as an opportunity to release some of the detainees from the internment centers and prepared a companion questionnaire, titled "Application For Leave Clearance" to be filled out by all camp inmates over age 17. As it turned out, the "loyalty" or "disloyalty" of the Japanese-American internees depended principally on their answers to Questions 27 and 28. Question 27 asked the internees if they were willing to serve in the armed forces of the

United States. Number 28 asked whether they would swear unqualified allegiance to the United States, and foreswear allegiance to the Japanese emperor and to any other foreign government.

For a variety of reasons too involved to discuss here, the "loyalty questionnaire" further fragmented the relations of the internees with their families and relatives, and even their friends. As an outcome of this ill-advised policy, by the fall of 1943, Tule Lake (located near the Lava Beds National Monument close to the California/Oregon border) had been converted from a concentration camp to a maximum security segregation center. As the WRA expected, the number of "disloyal" internees who had not answered the questionnaire were many. Arrival of these internees from other concentration camps began in autumn and by fall of the following year, Tule Lake was the largest of the ten centers, its population peaking at 18,000.

The segregation center comprised an area of more than 26,000 acres of sandy soil of a dry lake bed covered with tule reed. The region was arid and averaged only ten inches of rain annually. In the summer, the temperature often reached 100°F and in winter, which generally arrived relatively early, thermometer readings frequently dropped to -20°F.

The "camp," as it was sometimes called, was entirely surrounded by a high barbed wire fence with guard towers spaced at regular intervals, each manned and equipped with a searchlight and machine gun. In addition, within the center but outside the detainee area, there was a large fenced-in space where a battalion of military police and a number of army tanks were kept for "security duty." Tule Lake, as well as each of the other ten centers, had a project jail or similar enclosed area where draft resisters, NO/NO boys, and the like were confined.

Following the so-called November 4, 1943 WRA Food Warehouse incident, three innocent internees were detained as suspects by the WRA Security Guards. These unfortunates were subjected to an all-night investigation which entailed being brutally beaten to make them "confess." Then, without any medical attention, they were turned over to Army Security.

They were confined to an army tent from November 4, 1943 to early 1944 and were issued only metal cots, placed on the bare ground, and two army blankets each to ward off the frigid cold. This tent area, located in a double-fenced compound, became known as the "Bull Pen" and was situated close to the Tule Lake Hospital referred to as Area B.

Martial law was declared soon afterward and barracks were hastily constructed to house the increasing number of "suspects" and so-called "trouble-makers" who, by the spring of 1944, numbered close to 300. Ten months later, the last 18 inmates were released and what had become known as the Tule Lake Stockade was razed overnight. What remains now is only the Men's Project Jail.

Many touching Haiku, included in this anthology, were written during this period.

Another section of Tule Lake comprising almost 3,000 acres was set aside for farm operations outside the Center, euphemistically called the "colony." Here, some of the internees, always under guard, grew vegetables for their own camp, for its military garrison, for other camps, or for various Army and Navy units. As with other centers, Tule Lake paid internees $12, $16, or $19 monthly, depending on whether they were farmers, technical personnel or highly-skilled professionals.

In order to make their lives more bearable, the internees tried to keep their personal routines and their lives as "normal" as possible. They commemorated religious and cultural holidays, participated in baseball games and other sports, tried to make Japanese gardens near their living quarters, and exchanged seeds and plants to embellish their particular areas as much as possible.

They also held poetry meetings where they read their haiku, in which they expressed their hopes and plans to reshape their post-war lives in America (or Japan, if they returned there).

In 1979, a plaque with the designation "California Historical Landmark No. 850–2" was placed where the main entrance to Tule Lake had been located. In recent times, a yearly tour called "Tule Lake Pilgrimage" is arranged by Japanese-American organizations. Tourists and former internees alike continue to have difficulty believing that such a concentra-

Castle Rock Mountain. Tule Lake from administration housing area.

tion camp could have existed in the United States, let alone in California, only half a century ago—at the same time that our own great democracy was locked in a life and death struggle with Adolph Hitler's evil dictatorship.

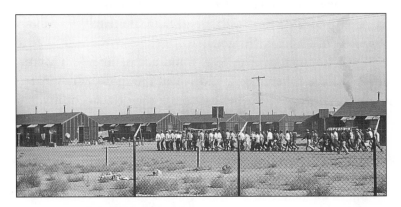

Tule Lake Segregation Center scene.

Internee barracks at the Tule Lake Segregation Center. Castle Rock Mountain in left background. Oil painting by internee artist S. Mikami.

69

Although in the fall of 1942 most of the internees of the Fresno and Stockton Assembly Centers were sent to Jerome and Rohwer, some detainees were moved to the Gila Concentration Camp located near Gila Bend, approximately 60 miles southwest of Phoenix, Arizona.

In the summer of that year, hundreds of internees were found to have tuberculosis, and it was thought the dry Arizona climate would be beneficial to their health. Accordingly, those who were infectious were sent to the sanatorium at the Gila Indian Reservation for treatment, and their families and detainees from other centers were interned in the nearby Gila Concentration Camp.

One of the better-known internees sent to the Gila Indian Reservation for treatment was Neiji Ozawa, the haiku master and founder of the Valley Ginsha Haiku Kai. In the more than two years he spent at Gila Hospital, Ozawa wrote many poems—some lamenting his grievous illness and the death of patients who had become his friends, as well as the desert scenery, the frequent dust storms, the stark appearance of sagebrush and saguaro cactus, and the beauty of the desert sunsets.

For all of its surrounding beauty, the Gila Concentration Camp was far from a beautiful place to live for its population, which was reported to have peaked at 13,000. In the summer, it was not unusual for the temperature to reach 130° F (55° C) and the occasional choking dust storms were terrifying to those internees not used to them.

As the War progressed, agricultural workers, attracted by the prospects of better paying jobs, migrated to the cities. Because of this, a farm crisis developed in the Arizona cotton fields and the US Government decided to use the internees to work in those fields. Eventually a large number of camp inmates ended up helping to avert an agricultural disaster in the Arizona cotton fields, similar to other internees' efforts which saved the sugar beet crops in Utah, Idaho, Montana and Wyoming.

Those assigned to harvest the cotton were trucked daily to the fields where they worked long, exhausting hours in the scorching desert sun. In the evening, they were trucked back to camp. It was a hard life for those who had come from the more moderate climate of California, and many internees felt that they were exploited by the WRA. In spite of their arduous life, internees composed songs and ditties to uplift their spirits. One such, still being sung by former Gila internees at their gatherings, is:

HILA NO MEIBUTSU KAZU ARE DO
SUZU HEBI, KAKUTASU, SASORI
CHOITO NEE-SAN, KIO TSUKENA
DAIKON ASHI NI KIZU GA TSUKU

which, freely translated, reads:

Gila has many well-known attractions—
rattlesnakes, cactuses, scorpions
But just a minute miss—be careful or
the pudgy white leg will be injured.*

*(Alternate)
But just a minute miss—be careful
the pudgy white leg is not injured.

Department of Justice Detention Camps for Enemy Aliens: Lordsburg, Santa Fe, Crystal City, and Missoula

The Naturalization Act of 1790, reinforced by the US Supreme Court decision of 1922, denied naturalization rights to the Issei and subordinated them to alien non-citizen status, regardless of the length of their residence. For that reason, they were viewed in pre-war days as "legal resident aliens."

A presidential directive of September 1939 authorized the Federal Bureau of Investigation to draw up lists of individuals to be taken into custody in wartime. Thus, immediately after the Japanese attack on Pearl Harbor in 1941, the Justice Department activated its pre-war contingency plan to control enemy aliens and within 24 hours of the attack, 1,212 Japanese, mostly Issei, had been arrested and confined.

Who were the "potential troublemakers" who had been arrested? For the most part, they were the intellectuals—newspaper editors and correspondents, Buddhist priests, professionals and community leaders who might conceivably organize a "fifth column" to sabotage or hinder America's war efforts—or others who might have contributed to various organizations in Japan and, therefore, were suspect. Incidentally, the so-called unreliables arrested included about 50 seal and whale-hunting half-Indian and half-Eskimo Alaskan Japanese, some of whom met Japanese Americans for the first time in the internment camps.

The courts held that such arrests were not subject to the due-process clause of the Fourteenth Amendment to the US Constitution or to review by habeas corpus, and neither was it considered necessary by the authorities to disclose specific grounds for the arrests.

But the Issei who had been arrested were loyal, law-abiding and industrious citizens who had raised their American-born children to honor and respect America, the country of their birth. It is worthy of note that at no time did Army or Navy Intelligence have any cause to suspect the Japanese Americans of disloyalty, and that even J. Edgar Hoover, the director of the FBI, came to believe that the clamor for evacuation was "based primarily upon public political pressure than upon factual data." As a matter of fact, beginning on January 6, 1942, about one month after the Pearl Harbor attack, California legislators began urging the removal of all Japanese, aliens and citizens alike, from the West Coast. And, on February 19, President Roosevelt signed Executive Order 9066, authorizing the removal of all Japanese from the Pacific Coast states.

As time went on, the Justice Department organized a number of camps, but the majority of haiku included in this anthology is from the inmates of Lordsburg and Santa Fe. Lordsburg was located at an elevation of approximately 4,000 feet in the Pyramid Mountains of southeastern New Mexico, a short distance from the Arizona border. The Santa Fe camp was at an elevation of approximately 7,000 feet in the western foothills of the Sangre de Cristo mountains, near the city of that name in north-central New Mexico. Because the two camps were similar in many respects, a brief description of the latter should suffice for both.

By March 1, 1942, Santa Fe had been selected by the Justice Department as the site of one of their detention camps and by June 1945, the maximum number of internees was 2,100. The camp was surrounded by a 10-foot wire fence, topped by a two-foot barbed wire overhang, with guard towers and search lights at frequent intervals. Housing was adequate, but not comfortable. Food items typical of the Japanese diet were often unavailable and although the fare provided a balanced diet, it was generally tasteless, dull and monotonous—until a vegetable garden and a small poultry farm were started by the detainees to supplement their diet.

Although the Justice Department regulations prohibited brutality, force and violence, the guards tended to view the all-male inmates as dangerous; consequently, they tended to be more cruel and insensitive than the guards at concentration camps and, occasionally, the detainees were subjected to various types of abuse, including physical threats and beatings.

In addition to the routine maintenance work the detainees were required to perform, as did inmates in prisoner of war (POW) camps, they could also volunteer to do work not connected with camp upkeep and were paid at the rate of eighty cents for an eight-hour day.

As a result of being deprived of their liberty, heterosexual companionship, and being subjected to a reduction of foods and services (including lack of correspondence from their wives and families which was always censored and even, at times, withheld), many internees sought comfort in their haiku. They wrote about the inhospitable land or the beauty of the brilliant sunlight on the snowy landscape, the longing for their homes, wives and families, and their hopes for an early end to the War.

The truths the Issei were attempting to express in their haiku were the disillusionment and disappointment at being interned as "enemy aliens" when, in reality, they were aliens only because the discriminatory laws had denied them citizenship and full acceptance because of their Japanese ancestry.

Today, most of the Issei are gone and, with the exception of a few strands of rusting barbed wire or an occasional deteriorating building foundation at former interment centers, there is little to help us recall the past. At the site of the former Santa Fe Justice Department camp, there now stands the Santa Fe Sheraton complex with a parking area covering the location where my family members and friends were once detained.

Former Santa Fe Justice Department Camp site, now part of the parking lot of the Santa Fe Sheraton Hotel Complex.

Tule Lake internees, including American-born citizens, were usually rounded up during the night, and shipped to Santa Fe and other Justice Department camps.

Delta Ginsha Poets

Delta Ginsha poets submitted more than 2,000 haiku for critique during their six-month detention in the Stockton Assembly Center (May to November 1942). Of the total number of poems presented, Kyotaro Komuro, editor and leader of the Delta Ginsha, was forced by space restrictions to select only 525 haiku for publication in Volume I of the Delta Ginsha Haiku Collection, published as a supplement to the *Rohwa Jiho Sha*, the Rohwer camp newspaper.

In the course of their 13-month detention at Rohwer (November 1942 to December 1943), the members of Delta Ginsha celebrated their 100th haiku meeting. In December of the following year, more than 1,000 of their selected haiku, including some which had been written in diary form during the arduous trip from Stockton to Rohwer, were also edited and published in Volume II of the Collection. Both volumes were hand stenciled and mimeographed, and are now brittle and yellowed with age.

Among the poems published in these volumes were many written by members who had been arrested by the FBI before the internment had even begun, and who were interned in Justice Department detention camps for so-called enemy aliens.

In the fall of 1943, many of the internees from various internment centers, including Rohwer, were transferred to Tule Lake Segregation Center, where they organized the Tule

Lake Valley Ginsha and continued to write poetry, most of which was published by the *Utah Nippo.*

Following the closure of the internment centers at War's end, some of the former Delta Ginsha poets returned to Stockton and, along with more recent members, continued to write haiku. But, at its last meeting in May 1966, the Delta Ginsha Haiku Kai was finally disbanded because of the ill health of many of its older members and the lack of a qualified leader.

Stockton Delta Ginsha Group Photo (1938) at Brentwood (San Francisco) Picnic

Top Row (*left to right*): *Yajin Nakao, Izumi Taniguchi, Isamu Taniguchi, Reverend Ouchi, Togo. The four women are relatives of Yotenchi Agari.*

Middle Row (*left to right*): *Mr Fujita, Grandfather Taniguchi, Reverend Iwanaga, Tojyo Fujita (hat with flowers), Mrs Akimoto, Kikuha Okamoto, Hatsuho Komuro, Mrs Agari, Mrs Agari's mother, Takako Tsunekawa, Kaname Iwahashi.*

Bottom Row (*left to right*): *Yajin Kuwahata, Senbinshi Takaoka, Unidentified, Ryokuin Matsui, Shiho Okamoto, Jun Komuro, Kyotaro Komuro, Mr Ijuin Kiino, Yotenchi Agari, Kuhei Kushida*

Hand-Painted Postcards
Announcing the Monthly Delta Ginsha Haiku Meetings
Illustrated and written by Senbinshi Takaoka

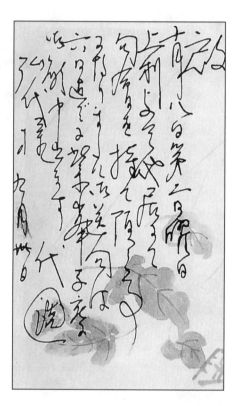

Announcement on September 30, of October haiku meeting. (Brown leaves symbolize the fall season.)

Announcement of May 31 haiku meeting. Card requests that contributors' haiku be submitted by the 18th. (Flying carp symbolize the Boys' Day Festival held yearly on May 5th.)

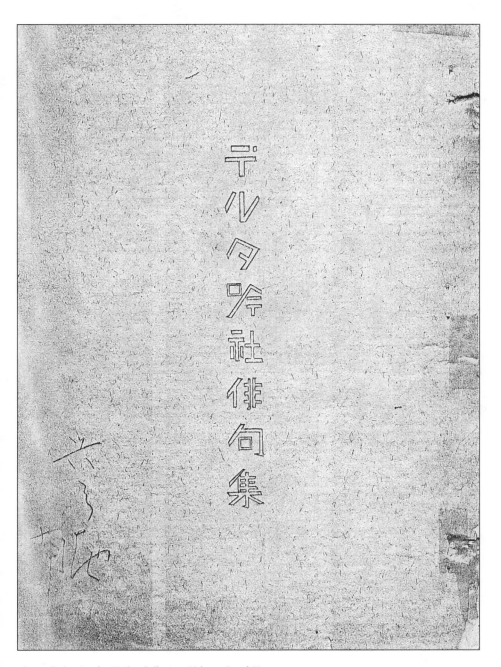

Cover, Delta Ginsha Haiku Collection, Volumes I and II

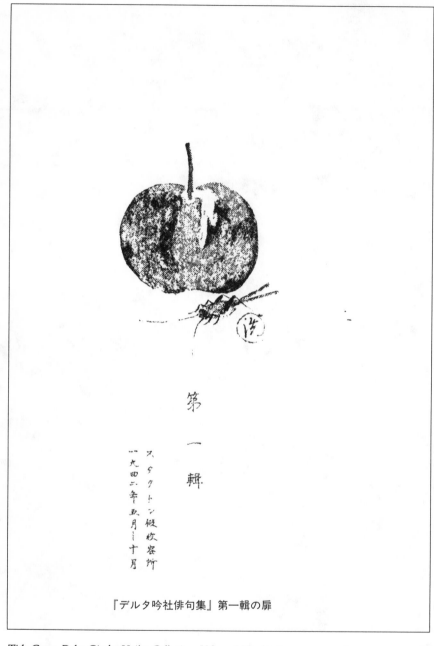

第　一　輯

ス　タ　ク　ト　ン　假　收　容　所

一九四二年五月〜十月

『デルタ吟社俳句集』第一輯の扉

Title Cover, Delta Ginsha Haiku Collection, Volume I (Stockton)
May – October 1942

ロ
丨
ア
転
住
所
の
一
年
.

自
一
九
四
二
年
十
一
月

至
一
九
四
三
年
十
二
月

第
二
輯

Title Cover, Delta Ginsha Haiku Collection, Volume II (Rohwer 1944)
November 1942 – December 1943

千九百四十一年五月十日吾々がスタクトンのアッセンブリ・センターに追入り鉄柵の内の生活を始めてから同年十月十七日に敵役にアカンソー州桐和転住所に移さるるまで五ヶ月余の間に二十回の句会を持った

句会での出句は毎会約百句内外で二十句に達してゐる。本稿はその中から選んだ同人作品の結晶である

一句一句の完不完は別として総ては吾々が仮牧容所に於ける暗い生活の記録であり、作品全部を載録すべきであるがそれは到底出来ない事である。僭越であるが私が推薦させて頂いた。

推薦に当っては所内に於ける吾々の生活に則したものに重点を置き見つ作者の個性は充分に尊重したつもりである。

鏡 太郎

Introduction to Volume I by Kyotaro Komuro (Stockton 1942)

Summary of Kyotaro Komuro's
Introduction to Volume I,
Stockton Assembly Center Haiku
May to October 1942

During the five months of incarceration at the Stockton Assembly Center (California), from May 10, 1941 [sic] to October of the same year (1942) when we were removed to the Rohwer Concentration Camp in Arkansas, we held twenty haiku meetings.

At each one of them about one hundred haiku were submitted, approximately 2,000 poems in all. From these voluminous writings diligent selection was made, and the best specimens make up this issue.

Since it is impossible to include all the haiku written at this camp, I took it upon myself, presumptuous as it may seem, to select those verses which best depict the individuality of each writer, the living conditions in the camp, and the hopes and disappointments of the internees in captivity.

Kyotaro

今や全世界全人類の総ゆる努力はすべて戦争の為めに費されてゐる

戦争は抑圧ではない。人間の常識を以て割り切れる出来事ではない

我々が夢想だにしなかつた加州の立退き、そしてアーカンソーの避地に欲柳内

の生活をつづける事も又戦争の一部でしかない

こうした生活の中にあつて独り自然と共に超然たり得る道は詩の世界の暮し

である。私達は俳句詩の世界に生きて行く幸福を感謝しなくてはならない。

一九四二年五月より九月まで、タクトン假集合所半砂の收穫を以て第一輯を

得て公にした。本輯は一九四二年十月アーカンソーに移つて以来一九四三年

十二月に至る一ケ年の收穫を収めたものである。

一九四四年九月

鏡　太郎　記

Introduction to Volume II by Kyotaro Komuro (Rohwer 1944)

Summary of Kyotaro Komuro's Introduction to Volume II, Rohwer Concentration Camp Haiku November 1942 – December 1943

Now all mankind's efforts are exerted toward the war. It is beyond one's comprehension or rationalization, but war is not based on reason.

Who ever dreamed we would be forcibly evacuated from California, and confined in this desolate area of Arkansas, surrounded by a barbed wire fence? This, too, is a facet of war.

In order for us to transcend our condition we must immerse ourselves in nature, and be grateful to find happiness in the life of haiku poetry.

Having compiled and published the haiku written at the Stockton Assembly Center in Volume I, the present Volume II is the fruit of our labor of love, written from October 1942 to December 1943, after our deportation to Arkansas.

Recorded by Kyotaro
September 1944

Biographical Notes

AGARI, YOTENCHI, *alternate leader who succeeded Komuro*
A native of Yamaguchi Prefecture, he came to America in
1915 and settled in Central California, where he became one
of the original chrysanthemum (mum) growers.

Agari and Neiji Ozawa met and subsequently became friends
when Ozawa moved to Stockton in 1917. The following year,
Agari attended the first Delta Ginsha Haiku Kai meeting, which
was held at Ozawa's home, and became one of its charter
members. In 1929, Agari attended the joint conference of the
Delta Ginsha/Valley Ginsha societies.

Agari was interned in the Stockton Assembly Center in
May 1942, and in October of that year was moved to the
Rohwer Concentration Camp. Most of this productive writer's
wartime poems were included in Volumes I and II of the Delta
Ginsha Haiku Collection (hereafter "the Collection") because
they touched the soul of the reader and poignantly described
the camp experiences of the internees.

Upon his release from Rohwer, Agari relocated to Den-
ver, Colorado; he eventually returned to Stockton, however,
to manage a fertilizer supply store. More importantly, though,
Agari reorganized and led the Delta Ginsha. Its prominence
was due, in large measure, to Agari's leadership, personality,
sagacity and sensitivity, and he became known among his col-
leagues as the "core person of Delta Ginsha."

While in his early seventies, Agari underwent three cancer operations. His friend Ozawa, in a moving tribute and "get well" message which he called "Don't Die Yotenchi," praised his invaluable contributions and enumerated some of the many reasons why Yotenchi should strive earnestly to overcome his illness and continue his productive life.

Agari continued to preside at meetings of the Delta Ginsha, but his illness relentlessly exacted its toll; residing in Stockton, he died in June 1962 at the age of 72.

Tanzaku

Haiku may be portrayed in a style called *Tanzaku,* written and signed in elaborate calligraphy on ornamented strips of cardboard, and are very suitable for display. Yotenchi Agari wrote often in the Tanzaku style.

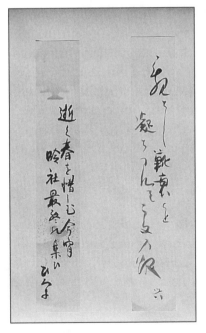

(L) *By Yotenchi Agari*

To the green mountain
casting the parting
fish line

(R) *By Hiroyo Takaoka*

Regret passing of spring
this evening gathered
at last poetry meeting

The haiku Agari wrote prior to his death seems to forecast his impending demise.

WAGA MI NO KAREYUKU SAMA GA MIE SOTO WA KANKAN HIGATERI

我が身の枯れゆくさまが見え
外はかんかん陽が照り

I can see myself withering
oppressive heat
outside sun is blazing

FUJITA, TOJO

All that is known about her is that she attended the first combined Delta Ginsha/Valley Ginsha Joint Conference in 1929. During the War, she was interned in the Stockton Assembly Center and later moved to the Rohwer Concentration Camp. She died in Stockton soon after the end of the War. Her internment haiku appeared in Volumes I and II of the Delta Ginsha Haiku Collection.

FUKUDA, HISAO

He was originally detained at the Missoula Justice Department Camp in Montana and was later moved to the Rohwer Concentration Camp. In 1943, he was relocated to the Tule Lake Segregation Center. A prolific writer, his early haiku was published in Volumes I and II of the Collection, and his Tule Lake haiku was published by the *Utah Nippo* in 1944. After the War, he did not submit any haiku to the Delta Ginsha meetings, and his whereabouts are unknown.

HIRAI, TOKUJI
His Rohwer haiku was published in Volume II of the Collection. (See also the biographical data under Tule Lake Valley Ginsha poets.)

IGUCHI, RYONAN
This poet wrote many of his haiku in the style of a diary, describing his trip from the Stockton Assembly Center to the Rohwer Concentration Camp. His poems were published in both volumes of the Collection. He moved to Denver, Colorado after the War, and attended the Denver Delta Ginsha meetings in 1945.

KANOW, SOICHI
He attended the first Delta Ginsha meeting at Ozawa's home in 1928. The following year, he attended and submitted his haiku at the Delta Ginsha/Valley Ginsha Joint Conference in Stockton. The haiku he wrote at the Stockton Assembly Center was published Volume I of the Collection, but none of his poetry appears in Volume II.

KOYAMA, KIDO
Some of the haiku he wrote while detained at the Stockton Assembly Center was published in Volume I of the Collection.

Kume, Seioshi

Nothing is known about this poet except that her very descriptive haiku, written at the Stockton and Rohwer centers, was published in both volumes of the Collection.

Kunimori, Honjyoshi

He was a charter member of the Delta Ginsha. He wrote profusely during his internment at the Stockton and Rohwer centers and his haiku was published in Volumes I and II of the Collection. At Rohwer, his job was a woodcutter, and his haiku about woodcutters and their labors express his feelings of futility and solitude. He submitted haiku at the Denver Delta Ginsha meeting in 1945. He died in Japan sometime during the 1960s.

Matsui, Ryokuin

Matsui was a charter member of the Delta Ginsha Haiku Kai. The haiku he wrote at the Stockton and Rohwer centers was published in both volumes of the Collection. He was said to be a severe and restrained person, and his feelings and camp experiences are logically expressed in his haiku. He died soon after the War.

Morimoto, Misen

The haiku he wrote during his internment at the Stockton Assembly Center, the Topaz Concentration Camp in Utah, and the Tule Lake Segregation Center was published in both volumes of the Collection.

NAKAO, YAJIN

He was born in Miyagi Ken (Prefecture), Japan in 1887 and came to the United States in 1907. He lived in Stockton prior to the War and became a charter member of the Delta Ginsha Haiku Kai. He was interned first at the Stockton Assembly Center and then at Rohwer Concentration Camp. His wartime haiku was published in both volumes of the Collection. Referring to his individualistic style of expression, Ozawa said Yajin was an adept and skilled old-timer at haiku writing—a well-deserved compliment. Nakao left the Rohwer Concentration Camp on November 30, 1945 and settled in the farming area of Modesto, Central California.

OKAMOTO, HYAKUISSEI

Very little is known about this poet beside the fact that about 50 of his haiku, including his well-written poems in the form of a "travel diary" covering his trip from Rohwer to Tule Lake in the fall of 1943, were published in Volume II of the Collection. After his arrival at the Segregation Center, he became active in the Tule Lake Valley Ginsha. (See also the biographical data on Valley Ginsha poets.)

OKAMOTO, KIKUHA (wife of Shiho Okamoto)

Her emotional haiku written during her internment at the Stockton and Rohwer centers and published in Volumes I and II of the Collection, laments the forced separation from her husband, who had been sent to the Justice Department Camp in Santa Fe at the beginning of the War. She died of a heart attack while at Rohwer on March 27, 1945.

OKAMOTO, SHIHO
He was born in 1888 in Wakayama Prefecture, Japan, and was a Delta Ginsha member for over 40 years. He was arrested by FBI agents in February 1942 and was moved to and from various camps, including Santa Fe and Lordsburg Justice Department Camps. While there, he wrote some significant haiku expressing his joy at the dignified behavior of the Japanese naval officers who had been taken prisoner after surviving the sinking of their carrier at the Battle of Midway, as well as his indignation over the needless shooting death of a recently-arrived detainee by a trigger-happy camp guard. Okamoto was later transferred to Rohwer, where many of his haiku were published in both volumes of the Collection. He died in 1967 at the age of 79.

OUCHIDE, KONAN
He was interned initially at Stockton where he worked in a mess hall, and then later relocated to Rohwer. His very descriptive haiku was published in both volumes. He moved to Nevada in January 1945.

OYAMA, YOSHIMATSU
A Methodist minister, he was interned at the Stockton Assembly Center. His poems appear in Volume I of the Collection. After the War, he moved to Chicago.

SHINTOMI, DAISHA
He wrote profusely while interned at the Rohwer Concentration Camp, and his haiku is included in Volume II of the Collection.

Suzuki, Shonan

His Stockton and Rohwer internment haiku was published in both volumes of the Collection. A productive writer, he later also attended meetings of the Tule Lake Valley Ginsha. He was a mild-mannered, lonely man who loved children. It is believed he repatriated to Japan after the War. (See also the biographical notes on Tule Lake Valley Ginsha poets.)

Takaoka, Hiroyo

She was born in Wakayama Prefecture, Japan in 1908. The only known survivor of the Delta Ginsha, she was interned at Stockton, Rohwer and Tule Lake. After the War, she relocated to Stockton, but now lives in San Jose where she is active in the senior citizen community. In the spring of 1991, she was visited by Haiku Master Mayumi Nakatsuka, son of the founder of the Kaiko Haiku School, and congratulated for the excellent haiku written by former members of Delta Ginsha.

Takaoka, Senbinshi (not related to Hiroyo Takaoka)

Considered a well-informed and artistic poet by his contemporaries, he illustrated many of the pre-war Haiku Kai meeting notices and cards, as well as the covers of Volumes I and II of the Delta Ginsha Haiku Collection (illustrated in this anthology). Many of his poems are also included in the volumes. Additionally, he wrote several highly-prized tanzaku for his friends. He was interned at Stockton and Rohwer, and in 1950 returned to Japan. He died in Kyoto.

TANIGUCHI, SADAYO (Miyagi)
She was born in Wakayama Prefecture, Japan in 1905. She married Isamu Taniguchi and immigrated to America in 1921. In 1925, she became a member of the Delta Ginsha, under the tutelage of Kyotaro Komuro. After being separated from her husband during her five-year internment, she was reunited with him at the Justice Department Camp in Crystal City, Texas. She stayed in Texas after the War ended. In 1977, her Tanka, entitled "Kyoshu" (Nostalgia) was published by Tanka Kenkyu Sha in Japan. Sadayo Taniguchi died in Austin, Texas.

TANIGUCHI, ISAMU
Like his wife, he was born in Wakayama Prefecture, in 1898. He first came to America in 1915, but returned to his native village to marry. In 1921, he and his wife immigrated to California where he resumed farming in the Brentwood area. Both he and his wife joined the Delta Ginsha in 1925.

On March 7, 1942, he was arrested by the FBI and for the next five years he and his wife were separated. Following their internment and subsequent reunification, they returned to California to resume farming. However, conditions were not what they had expected and Isamu and his family moved to the Rio Grande area of Texas, where his farming venture was, this time, a success. In 1963, he retired to nearby Austin where he died in February 1992.

TSUNEKAWA, HANGETSU
He was interned initially at Stockton and then at Rohwer. He wrote profusely, and many of his poems were published in Volumes I and II of the Collection. Following the War, he returned to Stockton.

TSUNEKAWA, TAKAKO
The wife of Hangetsu Tsunekawa, she was born in Nagoya City, Japan in 1892. Her haiku, written during her internment in Stockton and Rohwer, was published in both volumes. Many poems about her son, Lou, who was fighting in the European Theater of War, were included in the Collection. She died many years ago in Stockton.

YAMADA, JYOSHA
He was born in Aichi Prefecture, Japan on October 15, 1883. His wartime haiku, written while at Stockton and Rohwer, was published in both volumes of the Collection. Settling eventually in Stockton, he died on June 17, 1969 at the age of 86.

Haiku by Delta Ginsha Members During Internment

小室鏡太郎

スタクトンWRA集結センターにて

残暑道白し列し守られて行く日本人

屋根裏板と太い電線と明け易き

手紙を書く日があり暑き日をえらぶ如く

見張台仰ぐことなく行けり夏陽出る前

Komuro, Kyotaro
Stockton Assembly Center, May–October 1942

ZANSHO MICHI SHIROSHI RETSUSHI MAMORARETE YUKU NIPPON JIN

Lingering summer heat
Japanese proceeding under guard
on dusty white road

YANEURA ITA TO FUTOI DENSEN TO AKEYASUKI

Between ceiling slats
and thick electric wires
dawn comes through unhindered

TEGAMI O KAKU HI GA ARI ATSUKIHI O ERABU GOTOKU

Letter writing day
as if hottest day
had been chosen

MIHARIDAI AOGU KOTONAKU YUKERI NATSUHI DERUMAE

Passed guard tower
without glancing up
before summer daybreak

棚の木肌あつきに手をおき物を云へり

一卜日夏病む床のべに来て子

夫婦胡瓜数本を配るに紙につつみ

ローア強制収容所にて

水引く水にあそぶ子供等といたく

SAKU NO KIHADA ATSUKI NI TEO OKI MONOO IERI

Placing hand
on hot wooden fence—
talking!

HITOHI NATSUYAMU TOKONOBE NI KITE KO

Ailing one summer day
child comes
to bedside

FUFU KYURI SUHON WO KUBARU NI KAMI NI TSUTSUMI

Couple wrapping cucumbers
in paper
for sharing

Rohwer Concentration Camp, November 1942–December 1943

MIZUHIKU MIZUNI ASOBU KODOMORA TO ITAKU

Want to be with children
playing in water
of irrigation ditch

まこと音頭踊も独立祭も来し吾等に

裸で孫を抱かせて貫ふよろこび

ヒョウタンいくつもつるし黒い壁さむい風

庭にタキギつみ終りおなごたち去らず

MAKOTO ONDO ODORI MO DOKURITSUSAI MO KISHI WARERA NI

Indeed—festivals of
Obon and Independence Day
are here for us too

HADAKA DE MAGO WO DAKASETE MORAU YOROKOBI

Unclothed—
happy to be allowed
to hold grandchild

HYOTAN IKUTSUMO TSURUSHI KUROIKABE SAMUI KAZE

Many gourds hanging
on darkened wall
cold wind

NIWA NI TAKIGI TSUMI OWARI ONAGOTACHI SARAZU

Finished stacking firewood
in the yard
women linger

上利與天地

スタクトンWRA集結センターにて　一九四二年五月―十月

棲みて子を産みこの家去らんとす石楠花咲いてあるを

空に月ありて同じ家黒ふ並び立ち夏の夜

うら盆法会あり踊りあり収容所の星

馬場に住みくらす秋の篠懸芽が伸び

Agari, Yotenchi
Stockton Assembly Center, May — October 1942

SUMITE KO O UMI KONO IE SARANTOSU SHAKUNAGE SAITE ARUO

Rhododendron blooms
about to leave this house
where my child was born

SORA NI TSUKI ARITE ONAJI IE KUROU NARABI TACHI NATSU NO YO

Moonlit summer sky
same black houses
standing in rows

URABON HOE ARI ODORI ARI SHUYOSHO NO HOSHI

Obon Festival
services and dancing
stars over internment camp

BABA NI SUMI KURASU AKI NO SUZUKAKE ME GA NOBI

Fall—
still housed in stable
new sprouts on plantan tree

お婆さんは一人で死んだ鶏頭のはな

墓場には水もなからう今年盆がきた

ただに木を伐る事ばかり裸木の杜に

加州寒椿の夢うつつ咳をしつづけ

ローア強制収容所にて　一九四二年十一月—一九四三年十二月

OBASAN WA HITORIDE SHINDA KEITO NO HANA

Cockscomb flower
—alone—
elderly woman has died

HAKABANIWA MIZUMO NAKAROU KOTOSHI BON GA KITA

Festival of Souls
probably no water for them
in the cemetery this year

Rohwer Concentration Camp, November 1942–December 1943

TADANI KI O KIRU KOTOBAKARI HADAKAGI NO MORI NI

Cutting bare trees
only work to be done
in the forest

KASHU KANTSUBAKI NO YUME UTSUTSU SEKI O SHITSUZUKE

Dreaming
of California winter camellias
coughing all the while

あと、あと、あとに墓が出来地に水だまり

召され出る子の親々よ初雪降れり

ATO ATO ATO NI HAKA GA DEKI CHI NI MIZU DAMARI

Graves, another, and still another
on the ground
puddles of water

MESARE IZURU KO NO OYAOYA YO HATSUYUKI FURERI

Parents—
whose sons are called to the service
first snow falls

藤田藤女

スタクトンWRA集結センターにて

五月雨降りつづくバラックの窓顔がのぞき

夏草わづかふみ残されて吾等移動の話

ローア強制収容所にて

ともどち次ぎ次ぎ出所秋陽森に落ちる

汽車レールを軋る今宵思い出一年の秋夜

Fujita, Tojo
Stockton Assembly Center

SAMIDARE FURITSUZUKU BARAKKU NO MADO KAO GA NOZOKI

May rain continues
from the barracks windows
faces peer out

NATSUKUSA WAZUKA FUMINOKOSARETE WARERA IDOO NO HANASHI

Small patches
of untrodden summer grass
talk of our transfer

Rohwer Concentration Camp

TOMODOCHI TSUGI TSUGI SHUSSHO AKIHI MORI NI OCHIRU

Friends leave one by one
autumn sun
sets behind forest

KISHA RERU O KISHIRU KOYOI OMOIDE ICHINEN NO AKIYO

Train rumbles on track
this night memories of past year
autumn evening

115

福田久雄

福田久雄

モンタナ州ミゾラ司法省管轄強制収容所にて

仙人掌に刺あり花あり此の家高きにあり

哀れカウボーイの靴は曲り角を切らるる牛

ローア強制収容所にて

ただに軍用列車を見送る雪深く立ち

吹雪を行く我等に言葉なく鉄路の曲り

116

Fukuda, Hisao
Missoula, Justice Department Detention Center

SABOTEN NI TOGE ARI HANA ARI KONOIE TAKAKI NI ARI

On the cactus
there are thorns and flowers
this house is on a rise

AWARE KAUBOI NO KUTSU WA MAGARI TSUNO O KIRARURU USHI

Pathetic—
cowboys' boots are lopsided
cattle being dehorned

Rohwer Concentration Camp

TADANI GUNYO-RETTSHA O MIOKURU YUKI FUKAKU TACHI

Merely seeing off
troop train
standing in deep snow

FUBUKI O YUKU WARERA NI KOTOBA NAKU TETSURO NO MAGARI

Trudging through blizzard
no words spoken
railroad track curves

口笛をしては石をけりては歩く月見草咲き

一日てり一日吹き乾きたるポテトを拾う

お互い分らぬ言葉で笑ふ雪にぬれている顔

地の凍てひねもす伊太利人の長き外套

KUCHIBUE O SHITEWA ISHI O KERITEWA ARUKU TSUKIMISO SAKI

Walking and whistling
kicking pebbles
evening primrose in bloom

ICHINICHI TERI ICHINICHI FUKI KAWAKITARU POTETO O HIROU

Sunny day—
windy day
gathering dried potatoes

Working with Italian Prisoners of War

OTAGAI WAKARANU KOTOBA DE WARAU YUKI NI NURETE IRU KAO

Both sides laughing
not understanding the language
face wet with snow

CHI NO ITE HINEMOSU ITARI-JIN NO NAGAKI GAITO

Ground frozen
all day long
the long coats of the Italians

平井十九二

ローア強制収容所にて

斧かついで男杜ぎわの畠に何も見えない

児を叱る国訛り芥やく夏朝

蟬窓にきて鳴き木立に去りてなき

汽車の音きこゆ長き夜をさめてをり

Hirai, Tokuji
Rohwer Concentration Camp

ONO KATSUIDE OTOKO MORIGIWA NO HATAKE NI NANIMO MIENAI

Man carrying hatchet
in field near edge of forest
unable to see anything

KO O SHIKARU KUNINAMARI GOMI YAKU NATSUASA

Scolding child in native dialect
burning trash
summer evening

SEMI MADO NI KITE NAKI KODACHI NI SARITE NAKI

Cicada buzzing by the window
flew away to distant tree
continues to sing

KISHA NO OTO KIKOYU NAGAKI YORUO SAMETE ORI

Hearing sound of train
—AWAKE—
this endless night

井口嶺南

スタクトンWRA集結センターにて

馬場に起き伏して三月西瓜花咲き

ローア強制収容所にて

牛は腰骨とがつていて同じ形の箱汽車

牛は丸い目にじつと見ている荒野

遠く稲光りする暗に浮かびでる森

Iguchi, Ryonan
Stockton Assembly Center

BABA NI OKI FUSHITE MITSUKI SUIKA HANASAKI

Living, morning and night
three months in racetrack
watermelon flowers

Rohwer Concentration Camp

USHI WA KOSHIBONE TOGATTE ITE ONAJI KATACHI NO HAKOKISHA

Prominent backbone of cow
similar to row
of railroad boxcars

USHI WA MARUIME NI JITTO MITEIRU ARENO

Round eyes of cow
intently gazing
at barren land

TOOKU INABIKARI SURU YAMINI UKABI DERU MORI

Distant lightning flash
illuminates
dark forest

古山機堂

スタクトンＷＲＡ集結センターにて

軒下に高椅子五、六脚家に男五人なり

戴いて飲む一杯のブドウ酒パンもあつて秋晴れ

久米声応子

スタクトンＷＲＡ集結センターにて

何をかねがふ独立祭の一日を吾等

Koyama, Kido
Stockton Assembly Center

NOKISHITANI TAKAISU GO ROKU KYAKU IE NI OTOKO GO NIN NARI

Under the eaves
five or six high back chairs
there are five men in the room

ITADAITE NOMU IPPAI NO BUDOUSHU PAN MO ATTE AKIBARE

Gratefully drank glass of wine
there is bread also
clear autumn day

Kume, Seioshi
Stockton Assembly Center

NANIOKA NEGAU DOKURITSUSAI NO ICHINICHI O WARERA

We are hopeful
for something
this Fourth of July

草矢よくとび幾度かはなち小供

秋陽聴きに行く唄は日本の勝太郎

ローア強制収容所にて

黒人と手真似話しそこら毒草茂り

加能荘一

スタクトンWRA集結センターにて

人々腰かけていて日蔭の軒下浅く

126

KUSAYA YOKU TOBI IKUDOKA HANACHI KODOMO

Darts of reed travel far
children repeatedly
throw them

AKIHI KIKINI YUKU UTA WA NIHON NO KATSUTARO

Autumn evening
we go to hear
song of Japan's Katsutaro

Rohwer Concentration Camp

KOKUJIN TO TEMANE BANASHI SOKORA DOKUSO SHIGERI

Speaking to Negro
with hand gestures
poisonous plants growing all around

Kanow, Soichi
Stockton Assembly Center

HITOBITO KOSHIKAKETE ITE HIKAGE NO NOKISHITA ASAKU

People sitting
in the shade
under the narrow eaves

127

仄かなる地湿り仔雀二三羽は下りてわが戸口

初秋の白雲遙かに吾等に移動の話

国森本城子

スタクトンWRA集結センターにて

我等立退の日近く街にせんだんの花散りたり

人の多く語るなし一つの木陰にありて此の日

HONOKANARU CHISHIMERI KOSUZUME NI, SAN BA ORITE WAGA TOGUCHI

Slightly damp ground
two or three baby sparrows
descending in my doorway

SHOSHU NO SHIRAKUMO HARUKANI WARERA NI IDOO NO HANASHI

In the distance
early white clouds of fall
talk of transfers

Kunimori, Honjyoshi
Stockton Assembly Center

WARERA TACHINOKI NO HI CHIKAKU MACHI NI SENDAN NO HANA CHIRITARI

Our evacuation day nears
In the city
sandalwood flowers scattering

HITO NO OKU KATARU NASHI HITOTSU NO KOKAGE NI ARITE KONOHI

People not saying much
under the shade tree
this day

129

朝を少女走り夏草青き棚のあたり

ローア強制収容所にて

ぬかるみの靴のあとをふみ冬木冬木のたてり

自然はなしが立退きのことに秋の雨やまず

樹にいくばくか葉があり男已の行末を思ひ

130

ASA O SHOJO HASHIRI NATSUGUSA AOKI SAKU NO ATARI

In the morning girl runs
green summer grass
near the fence

Rohwer Concentration Camp

NUKARUMI NO KUTSU NO ATO O FUMI FUYUKI FUYUKI NO TATERI

Stepping on muddy shoe print
winter trees
yet standing

SHIZEN HANASHI GA TACHINOKI NO KOTONI AKI NO AME YAMAZU

Naturally,
talk of evacuation
fall rain continues

KINI IKUBAKUKA HA GA ARI OTOKO ONORE NO YUKUSUE O OMOI

Some leaves remain on trees
man anxious about
his own future

草枯れの道なり皺のまま長いコート

松井緑蔭

スタクトンWRA集結センターにて

打水にバラック総出となりハダシとなり

栅の外はハイウェーでありスズカケの葉はゆれ

ローア強制収容所にて

真夏食堂（メス）の鐘がなるよちよち歩む子

KUSAKARE NO MICHI NARI SHIWA NO MAMA NAGAI KOTO

Withered grass road
long coat
is still wrinkled

Matsui, Ryokuin
Stockton Assembly Center

UCHIMIZU NI BARRACKS SODE TO NARI HADASHI TO NARI

Sprinkling water outside
barracks occupants
in full force and barefooted

SAKU NO SOTO WA HAIUEI DE ARI SUZUKAKE NO HA WA YURE

Outside the fence is highway
leaves of plane tree
swaying

Rohwer Concentration Camp

MANATSU MESS HALL NO KANE GA NARU YOCHI YOCHI AYUMU KO

Midsummer
mess hall bell rings
tottering child

貧富の隔たりなくくらし暑いですなあ

夏夕べ舞台の人動く私等草原に座り

森本弥山

スタクトンWRA集結センターにて

導かるるまま穂草をふみ水をのみ

白菜味噌汁誰れとなく云へりぬくもりたり

HINPU NO HEDATARI NAKU KURASHI ATSUI DESU NA

Existing without barriers
between rich and poor
isn't it hot awfully hot?

NATSU YUBE BUTAI NO HITO UGOKU WATASHIRA KUSAHARA NI SUWARI

Summer evening
people moving on stage
we're seated on the grass

Morimoto, Misen
Stockton Assembly Center

MICHIBIKARURU MAMA HOGUSA O FUMI MIZU O NOMI

Following the lead
stepping on tall grass
and drinking water

HAKUSAI MISOSHIRU DARETONAKU IERI NUKUMORI TARI

Someone said
white cabbage miso soup
warms one up—it did

135

中尾野人

スタクトンWRA集結センターにて

往くも来るも箱庭のカンナのはな

労作箱一つ秋の短日

ローア強制収容所にて

師走雨戸口に並びたる小さい泥靴

冬眠の虫けら動くを火に入れる

Nakao, Yajin
Stockton Assembly Center

YUKUMO KURUMO HAKONIWA NO KANNA NO HANA

Whether one comes or goes
canna flowers
in the planter box

ROOSAKU HAKO HITOTSU AKI NO TANJITSU

Laboring—
over a box
short autumn day

Rohwer Concentration Camp

SHIWASU AMADOGUCHI NI NARABITARU CHIISAI DOROGUTSU

Year-end rain
in entrance way
row of small muddy shoes

TOMIN NO MUSHIKERA UGOKU O HI NI IRERU

Hibernating insect
twitching
cast in fire

国に帰りたくなった誰か待つやうで短夜

加州を偲ぶ

今は遠き国となり樹々紅葉す

部屋に二人住み人形一つが陽性の秋なり

つるとつる結びあひ咲いた朝顔の花

138

KUNI NI KAERITAKU NATTA DAREKA MATSU YODE TANYA

Want to go back to homeland
as if someone is waiting
short night

Reminiscing about California

IMA WA TOOKI KUNI TO NARI KIGI KOYO SU

Autumn foliage
California has now become
a far country

HEYA NI FUTARI SUMI NINGYO HITOTSUGA YOSEI NO AKI NARI

Two men sharing a room
only the doll looks real
it is fall

TSURU TO TSURU MUSU BI AI SAITA ASAGAO NO HANA

Vines entwine
morning glory flowers
blooming between them

物に慣れ居やすく樹々紅葉する

命あるもの異常あり朗和—雷、雨、風

岡本百一世

ローア強制収容所にて

木々伐ったあとはるかに人々焚火している

再転住の日は近し山柿の一と枝を折る

MONO NI NARE IYASUKU KIGI KOYO SURU

Getting used to things
feeling at ease
trees are turning crimson

INOCHI ARUMONO IJYO ARI ROUWA—KAMINARI, AME, KAZE

For living things
disorder
at Rohwer—thunder, rain, wind

Okamoto, Hyakuissei
Rohwer Concentration Camp

KIGI KITTA ATO HARUKANI HITOBITO TAKIBI SHITE IRU

After trees are cut down
in the distance
people making bonfires

SAITENJU NO HI WA CHIKASHI YAMAGAKI NO HITOEDA O ORU

Close to day of relocation
breaking branch
of wild persimmon

141

やがて去らんとする地の暑く棉畑実のり

岡本菊葉

スタクトンWRA集結センターにて

語りつつ看守塔にふりかへり夏夕べ

カンナの花が赤くどうする事もなく日々

往き来の車見てかり住ひの一夏もすぎやう

142

YAGATE SARAN TO SURU CHI NO ATSUKU WATABATAKE MINORI

Departing soon
ground is hot
cotton field near harvest

Okamoto, Kikuha
Stockton Assembly Center

KATARI TSUTSU KANSHUTO NI FURIKAERI NATSUYUBE

Chattering and glancing back
at guard tower
summer evening

KANNA NO HANA GA AKAKU DOSURUKOTO MO NAKU HIBI

Day after day
little to do
red flowers of canna

YUKIKINO KURUMA MITE KARISUMAI NO HITONATSU MO SUGIYO

Watched traffic go by
still in temporary quarters
summer is ending

143

別れて今日は一年庭の木瓜も咲いてよう

お国言葉の花種をうけ我が手のくぼ

朝顔ひいてしまひ旅立つ日せまり

岡本紫峰

一九四二年二月にFBIに検挙さる

引立てられて行く家に牡丹のつぼみかたし

Rohwer Concentration Camp

WAKARETE KYO WA ICHINEN NIWA NO BOKE MO SAITE IYO

Separated year ago today
Chinese quince
must be blooming in my garden

OKUNI KOTOBA NO HANADANE O UKE WAGATE NO KUBO

In my palm—flower seeds
you gave me
with their local names

ASAGAO HIITE SHIMAI TABITATSU HI SEMARI

Pulled out
morning glory vines
as day of departure nears

Okamoto, Shiho
Arrested by FBI February, 1942

HIKITATERARETE YUKU IE NI BOTAN NO TSUBOMI KATASHI

Being arrested—
at home peony bud
still firm

獄舎悲憤の一夜

ひとりで座りどす黒い壁を見つめ春の夜

サンタフェ司法省管轄収容所にて

日の出る尊さ山の一方に残る雪

食ふとねるほかなし雪降って地にきゆ

ローズバーグ司法省管轄収容所にて

夏の陽かげり番兵棍棒で石叩いている

146

One night in jail—Deploring Indignity

HITORIDE SUWARI DOSUGUROI KABE O MITSUME HARU NO YO

Sat alone staring
at dark and dismal wall
spring night

At Santa Fe Justice Department Detention Camp

HINODERU TOTOSA YAMA NO IPPO NI NOKORU YUKI

Majestic sunrise
on side of the mountain
snow lingers

KUU TO NERU HOKANASHI YUKI FUTTE CHI NI KIYU

Eating and sleeping
nothing to do
falling snow disappears into ground

At Lordsburg Justice Department Detention Camp, June 20

NATSU NO HIKAGERI BANPEI KONBO DE ISHI TATAITE IRU

In the shade of summer sun
guard tapping rock
with club

147

鉄柵動かない山から冬の日が出て

衛士の冬夜の暗さ衛士の口笛

日本海軍将士四十余名入所

一列の浅黄服粛然として秋の日

148

TETSUSAKU UGOKANAI YAMAKARA FUYU NO HI GA DETE

Iron fence immovable
over the mountain
winter sun rises

EISHI NO FUYUYO NO KURASA EISHI NO KUCHIBUE

Winter night
sentry whistling
in the darkness

Over 40 Japanese Naval Officers Enter Lordsburg Camp

(Between 40 and 50 Japanese Naval Officers, most of them survivors of the aircraft carrier Hiryu, *sunk at the Battle of Midway, were imprisoned at the Lordsburg Justice Department Camp in New Mexico, along with a few other POW's captured on Guam and the Aleutians.)*

ICHIRETSU NO ASAGIFUKU SHUKUZEN TO SHITE AKINOHI

Dignified military formation
even in POW clothing
autumn day

149

射殺されし二人の同胞を悼み

セーヂ原二つの新しい 土塚熱い 風吹く

ローア強制収容所にて

妻の死後、五ヶ月目の作

もの言はんにも一人春夜の窓をしめ

大内田江南

スタクトンWRA集結センターにて

日傘一つ馬場の曲りを通るひざかり

Mourning death of two brethren shot to death

SEIJI BARA FUTATSU NO ATARASHII DOZUKA ATSUI KAZE FUKU

In the sage brush
two new earth mounds★
torrid wind blows

Rohwer Concentration Camp
(Written in August 1945, after his wife died the previous March.)

MONO I WAN NIMO HITORI HARUYO NO MADO O SHIME

Even if I want to talk
I am alone
closed window, spring evening

Ouchida, Konan
Stockton Assembly Center

HIGASA HITOTSU BABA NO MAGARI O TORU HIZAKARI

A parasol goes by
along the curve of race-track
high noon

★ The mounds (graves) were for two critically ill internees who had just
arrived from a camp in Bismark, North Dakota, and were shot dead by
sentries who later alleged the two were "trying to escape from the camp."

子病みて小さき日輪草花をつけ

家ぬち氷わる音の外なし夏朝

むち鳴り薪馬車は少しぬかるみをいづ

クロンボー乗馬で行く綿畑の棉の花

152

KO YAMITE CHISAKI NICHIRINSO HANA O TSUKE

A child is ailing
tiny sunflower plant
with flowers

IE NUCHI KORI WARU OTO NO HOKANASHI NATSU ASA

In the house
only sound of chipping ice
summer morning

Rohwer Concentration Camp

MUCHI NARI MAKIBASHA WA SUKOSHI NUKARUMI O IZU

Crack of whip
lumber wagon begins
to creep out of mire

KURONBO JOBA DE YUKU WATABATAKE NO WATA NO HANA

Negro riding horse
cotton flowers
in the field

黒人棉を摘む丈低い棉の木

渡り鳥鳴く今朝咲く花の乏しく

大山義松

スタクトンWRA集結センターにて

ずうと馬場を歩いて誰れもついて来ない残暑

ローア強制収容所にて

児に誕生日近く長屋の庭葉げいとう目立ち

KOKUJIN WATA O TSUMU TAKE HIKUI WATA NO KI

Low cotton plants
black pickers
harvesting crop

WATARI DORI NAKU KESA SAKU HANA NO TOBOSHIKU

Migrating birds chirp
this morning blooming flowers
are scarce

Oyama, Yoshimatsu
Stockton Assembly Center

ZUTO BABA O ARUITE DARE MO TSUITEKONAI ZANSHO

Walked along the racetrack
no one followed
lingering summer heat

Rohwer Concentration Camp

KO NI TANJOBI CHIKAKU NAGAYA NO NIWA HAGEITO MEDACHI

Child's birthday nears
cockscomb by the barracks
showing vivid color

155

文書くにほのかなかほり林檎のかほり

新富泥砂

ローア強制収容所にて

月に凍て屋根のうす白きを帰る

今宵物々低い感じ春月のわが影

平和となる日を信ず啄木鳥を見上げず

156

FUMI KAKU NI HONOKANA KAORI RINGO NO KAORI

Writing letters
delicate fragrance
of apple scent

Shintomi, Deisha
Rohwer Concentration Camp

TSUKI NI ITE YANE NO USUSHIROKI O KAERU

Coming home
roof in whiteness
of icy moon

KOYOI MONOMONO HIKUI KANJI SHUNGETSU NO WAGAKAGE

This evening everything seems shorter
in spring moon
even my shadow

HEIWA TO NARUHI O SHINZU KITSUTSUKI O MIAGE ZU

Confident of peace to come
not looking up
at woodpecker

いつもの汽車すぎ又時計の音となる冬夜

鈴木湘南

スタクトンWRA集結センターにて　一九四二年五月―十月

蜘蛛のからだ動けり夏の日木陰のない家

大根芽が出た向き合ふてる表戸

真夏絵をかく薄い壁にささへられ部屋

158

ITSUMO NO KISHA SUGI MATA TOKEI NO OTO TO NARU FUYUYO

Usual train passes
sound of clock resumes
winter night

Suzuki, Shonan
Stockton Assembly Center, May–October 1942

KUMO NO KARADA UGOKERI NATSU NO HI KOKAGE NAI IE

Spider moved
summer day
house without tree shade

DAIKON ME GA DETA MUKI OTERU OMOTEDO

Radish sprouted
front doors (of barracks)
facing each other

MANATSU E O KAKU USUI KABE NI SASAERARE HEYA

Midsummer
drawing pictures
rooms thinly partitioned

草のあかるさ土堤ゆく鎌さげて女

としよりあけくれ庭木に水やる盆が近づく

長屋に住む裏も表も向日葵咲けり

別るる日のきまり残暑にたえている我等

Rohwer Concentration Camp, November 1942–December 1943

KUSA NO AKARUSA DOTE YUKU KAMA SAGETE ONNA

Light reflected by grass
walking on dike
woman with sickle

TOSHIYORI AKEKURE NIWAKI NI MIZUYARU BON GA CHIKAZUKU

Elderly persons watering garden plants
morning and evening
Obon festival is nearing

NAGAYA NI SUMU URA MO OMOTE MO HIMAWARI SAKERI

Living in barracks
front and back
sunflowers blooming

WAKARURU HI NO KIMARI ZANSHO NI TAETE IRU WARERA

Departure date set
enduring—
late summer heat

高岡広代

女五十半ば過ぎ昔の夢失はず持つ絵筆

もの縫ふウールの感触秋ふかみ

夕やけうすれゆく菊のつぼみの白きに佇ち

敬虔な想いに辞す門べ二十九年苔むす岩

Takaoka, Hiroyo
Delta Ginsha

ONNA GOJU NAKABA SUGI MUKASHI NO YUME USHINAWAZU
MOTSU E-FUDE

Woman past fifty
discards not dream of long ago
paint brush in hand

MONO NUU WURU NO KANSHOKU AKI FUKAMI

As I sew
I feel the woolen material
autumn deepens

YUYAKE USUREYUKU KIKU NO TSUBOMI NO SHIROKI NI TACHI

Fading sunset
standing by the whiteness
of chrysanthemum bud

Mourning Death of Agari Yotenchi

KEIKEN NA OMOI NI JISU KADOBE NIJUKUNEN KOKE MUSU IWA

Sympathetic thoughts
as I leave behind
rock with twenty-nine years' moss

感謝祭すぎ孤独に耐へて落葉掃く

高岡洗瓶子

スタクトンWRA集結センターにて

真夏のつばめを思ふ出入一方口の住ひ

夏夜何遍も繰返すレコード其れは支那の夜

衛兵立つ白壁の家夾竹桃咲けり

KANSHASAI SUGI KODOKU NI TAETE OCHIBA HAKU

Thanksgiving past
enduring solitude
sweeping fallen leaves

Takaoka, Senbinshi
Stockton Assembly Center

MANATSU NO TSUBAME O OMOU DEIRI IPPOGUCHI NO SUMAI

Midsummer
thinking of swallows
house with only one entrance

NATSUYO NANBEN MO KURIKAESU REKODO SORE WA SHINA NO YORU

Summer evening
repeatedly playing one record
it is "China Night"

EIHEI TATSU SHIRAKABE NO IE KYOCHIKUTO SAKERI

Sentry stands guard
whitewashed house
oleander blooming

夏夕地に図をかいて見せる男虹はつきり立ち

ローア強制収容所にて　一九四二年十一月―一九四三年十二月

霜夜汽車の轟をきく吾等遠く来しかな

小屋は冬枯のかぜ吹くにまかせ山羊鳴ている

霜朝の斧をわたされ今日木樵となる

NATSUYU CHINI ZU O KAITE MISERU OTOKO NIJI HAKKIRI TACHI

Summer evening
man sketching on ground
rainbow clearly set

Rohwer Concentration Camp, November 1942–December 1943

SHIMOYO KISHA NO TODOROKI O KIKU WARERA TOKU KISHI KANA

Frosty night
listening to rumbling train
we have come a long way

KOYA WA FUYUGARE NO KAZE FUKU NI MAKASE YAGI NAITE IRU

Winter wind
relentlessly blasting shed
goat bleating

SHIMOASA NO ONO O WATASARE KYO KIKORI TO NARU

Frosty morning
handed a hatchet
today I became a woodcutter

氷雨の夜を帰り釘に着物をかける

ローア強制収容所にて　一九四五年

西陽に落葉す我々の森の町

ゆめに通ふことの多くて秋夜

忍従三年夏朝の風吹く

HISAME NO YO O KAERI KUGI NI KIMONO O KAKERU

Returned at night
in icy rain
hung clothes on nail

NISHIBI NI OCHI-BASU WARE WARE NO MORI NO MACHI

Setting sun
leaves are falling
our quarters in the forest

YUME NI KAYOU KOTO NO OOKUTE AKI-YO

Dreams come and go
recurrently
autumn night

NINJU SANNEN NATSU ASA NO KAZE FUKU

Endured suffering
three years
summer morning wind

けだるさ単調の太鼓に更けて盆夜

谷口勇

テキサス州クリスタル・シティ司法省管轄強制収容所にて

夕日を惜しみて鳴く蟬の喧すさ家のまわり

冷蔵庫にメキシコマンゴ詰める国境近く住む我等

あれも譲りこれもゆづり我霜待つ秋野の芒

170

KEDARUSA TANCHO NO TAIKO NI FUKETE BONYA

Bored by monotonous drum
'till late hours
Obon festival night

Taniguchi, Isamu
Crystal City Justice Department Detention Camp

YUHI O OSHIMITE NAKU SEMI NO KAMABISUSA IE NO MAWARI

Distressed by setting sun
cicada chirps noisily
around the house

REIZOKO NI MEKISHIKO MANGO TSUMERU KOKKYO CHIKAKU
SUMU WARERA

In refrigerator
cramming Mexican mangoes
living close to border

ARE MO YUZURI KOREMO YUZURI WARE SHIMO MATSU AKINO NO SUSUKI

Bequeathed this and that
waiting for frost
pampas grass in autumn field

171

大いなる力に答ふ弱もののいくら祈っても冬が来る

谷口貞子

ローア強制収容所にて

遠くに友病むときく夕日にうなだれて日まわり

久遠の友の声聞くよう今朝の秋風

櫛にまつわる白き髪もわびしき秋朝

172

OOINARU CHIKARA NI KOTAU YOWAMONO IKURA INNOTTE MO
FUYU GA KURU

For puny individuals
futile to invoke higher powers
winter comes

Taniguchi, Sadayo
Gila Concentration Camp

TOOKU NI TOMO YAMU TO KIKU YUHI NI UNADARETE HIMAWARI

From far away heard
of friend's illness
sunflower drooping in setting sun

KUON NO TOMO NO KOE KIKU YOO KESA NO AKIKAZE

As if I hear
eternal voice of friend
this morning's autumn wind

KUSHI NI MATSUWARU SHIROKI KAMI MO WABISHIKI AKIASA

Coiled in comb
wretched gray hair
autumn morning

手錠され引かれゆく夫見送りしさま今日も目に見ゆ

ともに夫にはなれて一年はるか心はかすみ

テキサス州クリスタル・シティ司法省管轄強制収容所にて

国境ここにも二人の日系の墓あり土蟬の声

恒川半月

スタクトンWRA集結センターにて

収容所に来し夏夜バラックの灯一つ一つ

TEJYO SARE HIKARE YUKU OTTO O MIOKURISHI SAMA KYO MO
ME NI MIYU

Hand-cuffed and taken away
I see my husband
even today

TOMONI OTTO NI HANARETE ICHINEN HARUKA KOKORO WA KASUMI

Together, separated from husbands
already a year
heart veiled in mist

Crystal City Justice Department Detention Camp

KOKKYO KOKO NIMO FUTARI NO NIKKEI NO HAKA ARI DOSEMI NO KOE

At the border also
two Japanese-American graves
voice of mud cicada

Tsunekawa, Hangetsu
Stockton Assembly Center

SHUYOSHO NI KISHI NATSUYO BARAKKU NO HI HITOTSU HITOTSU

Came to internment camp
on a summer night
barracks lighting up one by one

正門の兵隊さんハッキリ顔に夕陽うけ

配給の靴土ついたまま土間におき西瓜食ふ

ローア強制収容所にて

冬の日子供らに海老がとれグラス瓶のせまい口

下駄材をすうすうけずるに極暑幾日

176

SEIMON NO HEITAISAN HAKKIRI KAO NI YUHI UKE

Sentry at main gate
face clearly exposed
in evening sun

HAIKYU NO KUTSU TSUCHI TSUITAMAMA DOMA NI OKI SUIKA KUU

Muddy issue–shoes
left on ground
eating watermelon

Rohwer Concentration Camp

FUYU NO HI KODOMORA NI EBI GA TORE GURASU BIN NO SEMAI KUCHI

Winter day
children catching shrimps
in narrow neck bottle

GETAZAI O SUU SUU KEZURU NI GOKUSHO IKUNICHI

Sound of man shaving wood for *geta*★
how many more days
of this extreme heat

★ Wooden sandal

わすれな草と思ふホースに口つけて水をのむ

恒川たか子

スタクトンWRA集結センターにて

ねむの若木繁り幼子小石とあそぶ

遠く雑音する夏夕手製の椅子にふかくかけて

戦地か演習か便りなし秋の夜半

178

Possibly a "forget-me-not" flower
drinking water
from the hose

Tsunekawa, Takako
Stockton Assembly Center

Small child
playing with pebbles
dense young silk tree

Distant noises
sat deeply in home-made chair
summer evening

Late autumn night
no news
battlefront or maneuvers?

来よ孫よここに一つの蟬のから

子供等西瓜を食べるに板道に腰かけて吾子も

山田篠舎

スタクトンWRA集結センターにて

片向月に我が影長し浴衣を着

窓掛の模様を知って片陰りの道を来り

Rohwer Concentration Camp

KOYO MAGOYO KOKONI HITOTSU NO SEMI NO KARA

Come here
grandchild—
this is a cicada shell

KODOMORA SUIKA O TABERU NI ITAMICHI NI KOSHI KAKETE AKO MO

Children eating watermelon
sitting on board walk
my child there also

Yamada, Jyosha
Stockton Assembly Center

KATAMUKIZUKI NI WAGA KAGE NAGASHI YUKATA O KI

Under the waning moon
my shadow is long
wearing *yukata*★

MADOKAKE NO MOYO O SHITTE KATAKAGERI NO MICHI O KITARI

Knowing pattern
of window curtain
came by shady road

★   Cotton robe

181

夏の朝風はつきりとして若葉の戦ひどき

桃の花雨やんだばかりの雫するさま

秋空黒雲忽ち覆ひ今日も来電に降られ

Rohwer Concentration Camp

NATSU NO ASA KAZE HAKKIRI TO SHITE WAKABA NO TATAKAIDOKI

Summer morning
wind blowing audibly
young leaves warring

MOMO NO HANA AME YANDA BAKARI NO SHIZUKU SURU SAMA

Peach blossom
rain just stopped
the sight of dew drops

AKIZORA KUROGUMO TACHIMACHI OOI KYOO MO RAI HYO NI FURARE

Black clouds instantly shroud
autumn sky
hail storming against us today also

Denson Valley Ginsha Poets

Biographical Notes

As earlier mentioned, much of the poetry generated by members of the Valley Ginsha Haiku Kai, under its leader Neiji Ozawa, was lost in the moves from one internment camp to another. Therefore, unfortunately, this anthology includes only a limited number of poems and biographies compared to what was offered from the Delta Ginsha poets.

Many of the internees initially relocated to the Fresno Assembly Center were later sent to Jerome Concentration Camp where they continued to have poetry meetings. Their club, the Denson Valley Haiku Kai, was an extension of the Valley Ginsha poetry club. Besides the biographical data, what follows is a sampling of the poetry which was generated at the "Farewell Haiku Kai" meeting shortly after the Camp closure was announced.

FUJIKAWA, YUKO
No information is available about this poet, except that she became a Valley Ginsha member while interned at the Jerome Concentration Camp in Denson, Arkansas, where one of her sons was a doctor in the camp hospital.

GOMYO, REIKO (*Pseudonym of Sadako Abiko*)
She was born in Shizuoka, Izu Peninsula, Japan. She became a charter member of Valley Ginsha on February 7, 1928, soon

after her arrival in Fresno. When she moved to the Los Angeles area in 1954, Ozawa deeply lamented her move and members of the Valley Ginsha were heartbroken, as what was left behind was an irreplaceable void. She lived in Los Angeles until her death on March 24, 1992. Her husband, Hiroshi Abiko, passed away just a few years prior to that. Their daughter, Yorko, still resides in Los Angeles.

Sadako was considered the outstanding haiku poetess of North America, who successfully incorporated an international flavor into her free-style haiku. When the haiku of this gifted poetess was included in the *Third Edition of the Free Style Haiku Collection,* published in Japan by the firm Kaizo Sha, her reputation was immediately established. With her distinctive form of expression, she influenced a number of orthodox poets, in Japan and elsewhere.

Many of her haiku were also published by the *Kaiko Journal* of Tokyo and by the Japanese-American newspapers before the War. Although, at times, her poetry was introspective and melancholic, it could also be elegant and sparkling; Ozawa called her haiku lyric and serene.

MOMOSE, ROSUI

A tailor in Fresno before the War, he occasionally attended the Valley Ginsha meetings. From the Fresno Assembly Center, he was transferred to the Jerome Concentration Camp. He returned to Fresno after the War, where he died.

NAKASHIMA, SHO

He was born in Kanagawa Prefecture, Japan in 1895. From the internment camp, two of his sons volunteered to serve in the War under the US Army. He returned to Fresno after the War and lived there until he died in 1984. He is buried at the Washington Colony Cemetery in Bowles, California.

One of the charter members of the Valley Ginsha, he also contributed to Tokyo's *Kaiko Journal*, continuing to do so until his death. This poet was long remembered by the Valley Ginsha members because of the fruits and vegetables he shared with them at the monthly meetings before the War.

OCHIAI, CHIYOKO
Although her haiku appears with the Denson Valley Farewell haiku, there is no information available about this poet.

SHINODA, YOUKO (*Pseudonym of Akiko Suda*)
She was born in Misasa Machi, Hiroshima City, Japan in 1899. A charter member of the Valley Ginsha, she was one of the foremost women haiku writers in the Central Valley. After her internment at the Fresno Assembly Center and at both the Jerome and Rohwer Concentration Camps, she returned to Fresno after the War. She died there on November 4, 1987, at the age of 90.

Haiku by Denson Valley Ginsha Members
During Internment

藤川幽子

野蒜ひっそり咲いて別れの日近づく

はなればなれに別れの日の夏の雲

五明玲子

おごそかそゝり立つ雪が嶺に向ひわれら

堪へよう眼にさみどりの淋しきいろを春を

192

Fujikawa, Yuko

NOBIRU HISSORI SAITE WAKARE NO HI CHIKAZUKU

Solitary bloom
of wild rocambole
day of departure nears

HANARE BANARE NI WAKARE NO HI NO NATSU NO KUMO

Departure day
families leaving one by one
summer clouds

Gomyo, Reiko

OGOSOKA SOSORITATSU YUKI-GA-MINE NI MUKAI WARERA

Majestic snow
on soaring peak
we face

TAEYO ME NI SAMIDORI NO SABISHIKI IRO O HARU O

Vision of loneliness
I endure
in the green of spring

夏の日ざし室に壁ありて昼をねむる

火事跡に立ちめいめい人間同志のことば

センター閉鎖発表、『ユタ日報』一九四四年七月十四日付

この日初蟬の声を聞くこの日草光る

溝べりこぞの草の芽が萌えてまた別れねばならぬ

NATSU NO HIZASHI HEYA NI KABE ARITE HIRU O NEMURU

Summer sunshine
room with partitions
sleeping in afternoon

KAJIATO NI TACHI MEI-MEI NINGENDOSHI NO KOTOBA

Standing at burned structure
each individual
speaking his own idiom

Center closure announced in Utah Nippo *July 14, 1944*

KONO HI HATSUZEMI NO KOE O KIKU KONOHI KUSA HIKARU

Today
the first cicada chirps
this day the grass glistens

MIZOBERI KOZO NO KUSA NO ME GA MOETE MATA WAKARENEBA NARANU

By the ditch—last year's grass
begins to bud
again we must part

何か襲はるごとき想ひ枯れがれ草密生す

加州帰還

芽ぶくその日のくるであらうまだ堅い樹のつぼみ見上げる

百瀬蘆水

雲は南に北に流れ一日初夏の空

中島正

じゃがいもの花も胡瓜の花も此地去らんとす

NANIKA OSOWARU GOTOKI OMOI KAREGAREGUSA MISSEI SU

Feeling of oppression
withering weeds
are dense

Return to California

MEBUKU SONOHI NO KURUDE AROO MADA KATAI KI NO TSUBOMI
MIAGERU

Firm buds will open
when the day comes
looking up at the trees

Momose, Rosui

KUMO WA MINAMI NI KITA NI NAGARE ICHINICHI SHOKA NO SORA

Clouds drifting day long
north and south
early summer day

Nakashima, Sho

JAGAIMO NO HANA MO KYURI NO HANA MO KONO CHI SARAN TO SU

Flowers of potatoes and cucumbers
also about to depart
from this place

197

青い林もやがてなごりのひとびと

子をつわものにゆかせ遙々セージ原にひとり

生きて息すれば息白し霜白し

落合千代子

初夏の夜の卓上の花であり風すこしあると

AOI HAYASHI MO YAGATE NAGORI NO HITO-BITO

Green forests in time
also bid farewell
to men

KO O TSUWANONO NI YUKASE HARU BARU SEIJI-BARA NI HITORI

Son joined the army
walked great distance
alone in the sagebrush

IKITE IKI SUREBA IKI SHIROSHI SHIMO SHIROSHI

Alive, as I exhale
breath is white
and frost is white

Ochiai, Chiyoko

SHOKA NO YO NO TAKUJO NO HANA DE ARI KAZE SUKOSHI ARU TO

Early summer evening
flower on table
slight breeze

篠田葉子

野茨咲くこの畠烈日の照りて

友に限りある日のきて地の草青し濡れて

空虚雀二三羽木がくれ鳴いて日ぐれ

Shinoda, Yorko

NO-IBARA SAKU KONO HATAKE RETSUJITSU NO TERI TE

Wild roses blooming
garden parched
blazing sun

TOMO NI KAGIRI ARUHI NO KITE CHI NO KUSA AOSHI NURETE

End of friend's life
has come
grass is green and wet

KUUKYO SUZUME NI-SANBA KOGAKURE NAITE HIGURE

Meaningless life
two or three sparrows chirping
hiding in the tree at sunset

Tule Lake Valley Ginsha Poets

After Tule Lake was designated a segregation center in 1943, many former Kaiko members from the Denson Valley Ginsha (Jerome), Rohwer Concentration Camp, and various other camps were relocated to this new center near the California-Oregon border.

By January 1944, these haiku poets had formed the Tule Lake Valley Ginsha. The haiku generated from Tule Lake was plaintive and, at times, defiant. As mentioned earlier, not only did the internees have to deal with the separation from friends and family (as a direct result of the "loyalty" questionnaire*), their situation was aggravated by the visits of some of the Nisei who had volunteered for military service—even by those who had done so against their fathers' wishes. In many cases, this was a "final separation" or a "fateful farewell" before being sent into combat. These visits, in turn, gave rise to a vigorous outpouring of haiku expressing the disappointment, frustration, and even indignation of the Issei who had remained behind barbed wire fences while their sons risked their lives for a country that continued to regard their parents as disloyal.

Haiku, however, was also written about the flowers they

---

* The "loyalty" questionnaire was an injudicious attempt by the war department to organize a volunteer combat team of Nisei soldiers.

grew or which grew in their locality, the geological land-marks easily visible from the camp—Abalone Mountain and Castle Rock, some of the disturbances which occasionally erupted in Tule Lake, and even about some of the trivial little things such as an insect or spider web—about anything which caught their attention or affected their lives. Some of the most touching wartime haiku was written during this period of incarceration.

As internees from other centers were transferred to Tule Lake, the haiku poets contacted each other, joined together in poetry meetings, and soon formed the Tule Lake Valley Ginsha. Poetry was submitted for critique at their monthly haiku meetings until December 1944, when many of the club's male members were moved to the Justice Department Camp in Santa Fe. Those internees continued to write poetry hoping it would eventually be put into the hands of their families and friends at Tule Lake and be included in the monthly poetry readings there. But the haiku was censored, and most of it was lost when those detainees were expatriated or repatriated to Japan at the end of the War.

Today, with the exception of myself, the haiku writers of the Tule Lake Valley Ginsha have all passed on, and their biographical notes are either scanty or entirely non-existent.

Sumie (*brush painting*) *of Castle Rock Mountain. Prominent Tule Lake landmark, drawn for Kazue Matsuda by Rhyuho Honda while both were interned at Tule Lake.*

Whole view of Tule Lake—Abalone Mountain in the background

Biographical Notes

HIRAI, TOKUJI
Very little is known about this poet, except that he began writing haiku after his arrival at the Rohwer Concentration Camp in late 1942. He continued his prolific output after his transfer to the Tule Lake Segregation Center in 1943. While there, his haiku was published by the *Utah Nippo,* the Japanese newspaper of Salt Lake City, in 1944, along with poems submitted by other Tule Lake Valley Ginsha members. An imaginative and sensitive poet, his haiku vividly expresses his wartime internment experiences.

MATSUDA, HEKISAMEI (Shigeru)
He was born in 1906 in Iimuro Mura, Asa-gun, Hiroshima Prefecture, and remained in Japan with his mother while his father immigrated to America. When Shigeru was in his teens, his father sent for him and his mother. While staying at the Fresno Buddhist Church dormitory, Shigeru participated in many church activities, including the literary discussion group, oratorical contests, dramatic plays, golf tournaments, photography contests, and haiku writing; he prided himself as the product of the Fresno Buddhist Church Youth Leaders Group.

He became a charter member of Valley Ginsha and while he and his family were living in Fresno, he also owned and managed the Matsuda Book Shop, taught in several Japanese language schools in the Central Valley, was a correspondent for various Japanese-American newspapers, and was in charge of Japanese theatrical performances in the Fresno area. The haiku he wrote at this time was published by the *Kaiko Monthly Journal* in Japan. After hostilities broke out, he was interned initially at the Fresno Assembly Center, then at Jerome Concentration Camp, and finally at Tule Lake Segregation Center. During that time, his haiku was published by the *Utah Nippo*. In December 1944, he was sent to the Santa Fe Justice Department Camp and the following December was repatriated to Japan, where he remarried. He died in late 1970.

MATSUDA, KAZUE (Violet Kazue de Cristoforo)
See "About the Complier," p. 283.

MATSUSHITA, SUIKO
No information is available about this poet, except that he became a member of the Tule Lake Valley Ginsha in 1944. His poems are well written and suggest he was familiar with the haiku tradition, but the melancholic and wistful style of his poetry intimate the dejection and desolation he must have experienced in life.

MORIMOTO, MISEN
He was interned in the Stockton Assembly Center in May 1942, Tule Lake in 1943, and later relocated to the Topaz Concentration Camp in Utah. He was a prolific writer and many of his poems were sent to Kyotaro Komuro. They were subsequently included in Volumes I and II of the Delta Ginsha Haiku Collection, and published in the Supplement of *Rohwa Jiho Sha,* the Rohwer camp newspaper, in December 1944.

OKAMOTO, HYAKUISSEI

He was interned at the Stockton Assembly Center, the Rohwer Concentration Camp in 1942 and, later in 1943, at Tule Lake. Many of his haiku were published in Volume II of the Delta Ginsha Haiku Collection and by the *Utah Nippo,* both in 1944.

SAGA, SHOKOSHI (*Pen name of Hideo Ito*)

He was born in Mie Prefecture, Japan. As well as being a charter member of the Valley Ginsha Haiku Kai, he was a Japanese language school teacher and a correspondent for a Japanese newspaper. He, too, spent years at Fresno, Jerome, and Tule Lake, but continued writing haiku throughout the War. Many of his poems were published by the *Utah Nippo* in 1944. He moved to San Francisco after the War and died there in the Spring of 1988.

SAGARA, SEI

This poet became a Tule Lake Valley Ginsha member in 1944 and, directly following that, had many haiku published monthly by the *Utah Nippo.*

SUZUKI, SHONAN

He was interned at Stockton, Rohwer, and at Tule Lake. A productive writer, many of his poems appeared in Volumes I and II of the Delta Ginsha Haiku Collection. In contrast with the poems he had written earlier, the somber haiku he wrote during his Tule Lake internment emphasize his deep solitude and sensitiveness. These poems were published by the *Utah Nippo* in 1944. After the War, it is believed he repatriated to Japan.

TAKEDA, SENBO (*Pen name of Sanichi Uyemaruko, husband of Shizuku Uyemaruko*)
He joined the Valley Ginsha in 1928. As well as being an active member of the Fresno Buddhist Church, he owned a bicycle shop in Fresno's "Japan Town." He died there after the War. His Tule Lake Valley Ginsha haiku was published by the *Utah Nippo* in 1944.

TATESHINA, BYOSO
Very little is known about this poet, except that he began writing haiku at Tule Lake in 1943. His poems were published by the *Utah Nippo* in 1944. His poetry suggests he was suffering from an incurable disease.

UYEMARUKO, SHIZUKU (*Pen name of Sachiko Uyemaruko*)
She was born in Mukainada, Hiroshima City, on August 15, 1898, and emigrated to America in 1917. A charter member of Valley Ginsha, until recently she contributed her haiku to the monthly *Kaiko Journal* of Tokyo. During the War, she was interned at the Fresno Assembly Center, Jerome Concentration Camp and at Tule Lake. Shizuku Uyemaruko declined to share with the compiler any biographical data or other information about her late husband, Senbo Takeda, other Valley Ginsha members, or even herself. She died in Fresno on October 4, 1992 at the age of 94.

WADA, HAKURO (*Also known as Kenji Wada*)
He was born in Stockton in 1916, but received most of his education in Japan prior to returning to America in 1937. He was interned in the Fresno Assembly Center, Jerome Con-

centration Camp, and at Tule Lake in 1943, where he became a member of a youth organization. He was then sent to the Justice Department Camp in Santa Fe and was later isolated at the Fort Stanton (New Mexico) Justice Department Camp. In 1944, while there, he became a member of the Tule Lake Valley Ginsha and some of his poems were published by the *Utah Nippo* in that same year. His haiku reflects his love and his longing for Japan. Hakuro Wada was expatriated to Japan in 1945.

*Haiku by Tule Lake Valley Ginsha Members
During Internment*

尾澤寧次

フレスノWRA集結センター入り　一九四二年五月十六日

幼きこほろぎとび黒き土間に馴るる

死別の感じ炎暑砂利ふんで君達去る

木陰にベッドを移し余命なき男眠り

アネモネの花病みてあれば国は遠い

Ozawa, Neiji
Entered Fresno Assembly Center May 16, 1942

OSANAKI KOOROGI TOBI KUROKI DOMA NI NARURU

Young cricket jumped
getting used
to dark mud floor

SHIBETSU NO KANJI ENSHO JARI FUNDE KIMITACHI SARU

Sensing permanent separation
as you left me in extreme heat
on gravel road

KOKAGE NI BEDDO O UTSUSHI YOMEI NAKI OTOKO NEMURI

Moved bed in shade of tree
man nearing end of life
sleeps

ANEMONE NO HANA YAMITE AREBA KUNI WA TOOI

Flower of anemone
motherland seems so distant
when one is ailing

いくさ加州を追われ砂漠の湖波たたぬ日

ヒラ強制収容所　インディアン居留地療養所にて

カクタス原ローカル・トレインぽっぽと走り

いくさ此の年除夜の鐘砂漠に鳴る

病歴語り合ひ一人眠り二人眠り冬の夜

IKUSA KASHUU O OWARE SABAKU NO MIZUUMI NAMI TATANU HI

War forced us from California
No ripples this day
on desert lake

At Gila Camp Hospital (Indian Sanatorium)

KAKUTASUBARA ROOKARU TOREIN POPPO TO HASHIRI

Cactus field
local train
huffing and puffing

IKUSA KONO TOSHI JOYA NO KANE SABAKU NI NARU

The war—this year
New Year midnight bell
ringing in the desert

BYOREKI KATARIAI HITORI NEMURI FUTARI NEMURI FUYU NO YO

Sharing medical histories
on a winter night
one by one we fall asleep

南国アリゾナ・サンセット雄大金色の雲動く

砂漠にも四季のながめネルの寝巻きに代え

鉄柵の中に生まれし子もまじり元旦

いくさは勝つものとして一世豆蔓の糸を張り

218

NANGOKU ARIZONA SANSETTO YUUDAI KINIRO NO KUMO UGOKU

Southern state—Arizona
magnificent sunset
golden cloud drifting

SABAKU NIMO SHIKI NO NAGAME NERU NO NEMAKI NI KAE

Even in the desert
four seasons are seen
changing into flannel nightshirt

TETSUSAKU NO NAKA NI UMARESHI KO MO MAJIRI GANTAN

Even babies born inside barbed wire fence
mingling—
on New Year's Day

IKUSA WA KATSU MONO TO SHITE ISSEI MAMEZURU NO ITO O HARI

For the Issei war is to be won
placing support
for string bean runners

あけて星は消え夢はどこへすてる

砂漠雨ふり喀血あとの眠りにおち

忍苦二年敵の国妻は大根干す

眞近く稲妻し山の方稲妻しガウン着ている

220

AKETE HOSHI WA KIE YUME WA DOKO E SUTERU

At daybreak
stars disappear
where do I discard my dreams?

SABAKU AMEFURI KAKKETSU ATO NO NEMURI NI OCHI

Desert rain falling
spitting blood
then fall asleep

NINKU NINEN TEKI NO KUNI TSUMA WA DAIKON HOSU

Enduring two year submission
in enemy (alien) nation
wife is drying *daikon*★

MAJIKAKU INAZUMA SHI YAMA NO HOO INAZUMA SHI GAUN KITE IRU

Lightning nearby
and on mountains
wearing hospital gown

★ Used in making pickled radishes, part of Japanese diet.

死期近き人と並び病み金盞花二人が見た

人逝きし翌朝の陽ざし立木の長い影

希望のない窓からさつきぞらあしたもある

遠く枯れし花に立ち涙にぶき音きこゆ

SHIKI CHIKAKI HITO TO NARABI YAMI KINSENKA FUTARI GA MITA

Ailing—
alongside dying man
we both looked at marigold

HITO YUKISHI YOKUASA NO HIZASHI TACHIKI NO NAGAI KAGE

Patient passed away
next morning sunshine
casts long shadow of tree

KIBOO NO NAI MADO KARA SATSUKIZORA ASHITA MO ARU

From the window of despair
May sky*
there is always tomorrow

TOOKU KARESHI HANA NI TACHI NAMIDA NIBUKI OTO KIKOYU

Standing afar
by wilted flower
tears trickled down

* Title of the present anthology.

223

松田一恵

同士そろふそして松の芽太り初夏の空

三ッ葉の花咲きし日々たしかに生きん

植物貧弱と思ふそここ夏の畑

紫うすきかつ葉がくれに折れし一輪

224

Matsuda, Kazue

DOOSHI SOROU SOSHITE MATSU NO ME FUTORI SHOKA NO SORA

Like-minded people gather
new shoots sprout from pine tree
early summer sky

MITSUBA NO HANA SAKISHI HIBI TASHIKA NI IKIN

Trefoil flowers bloom
daily—
I shall live positively

SHOKUBUTSU HINJAKU TO OMOU SOKO KOKO NATSU NO HATAKE

Vegetation seems meager
here and there
summer garden plots

MURASAKI USUKI KAKITSU HAGAKURE NI ORESHI ICHIRIN

A pale purple iris
on a broken stem
hidden under a leaf

ほうれん草は青きもの地より生へ一うねほうれん草

呼吸する朝太陽大きい総て親と子の真実

たんぽぽ、けている雨上がりの地を行く

女は男より忙しく雑然人住ふかきつばた

HORENSO WA AOKI MONO CHI YORI HAE HITOMUNE HORENSO

Spinach are green
one row growing
from the soil

IKISURU ASA TAIYO OKII SUBETE OYA TO KO NO SHINJITSU

Morning breath—huge sun
parent-child relationships
all based on trust

TANPOPO HOOKETE IRU AMEAGARI NO CHI O YUKU

Dandelion passed its peak
walking on ground
after the rain

ONNA WA OTOKO YORI ISOGASHIKU ZATSUZEN HITO SUMAU
KAKITSUBATA

Women are busier than men
people living in disarray
and there are Irises

時雨れる山々遠く静けし

地面人踏まぬ穂草のびひばりとぶ

素足で歩けそうもなく穂草つゞく

おろかしさたゞに夏の日をくらし向ふキャソルロック

SHIGURERU YAMA-YAMA TOOKU SHIZUKESHI

Winter shower
distant mountains
serenity

JIMEN HITO FUMANU HOGUSA NOBI HIBARI TOBU

Untrodden ground
grasses tall
skylark soars

SUASHI DE ARUKESO MO NAKU HOGUSA TSUZUKU

Seem unable
to walk barefooted
continuing tall grass

OROKASHISA TADA NI NATSU NO HI O KURASHI MUKOU CASTLE ROCK

Foolishly—simply existing
summer days
Castle Rock is there

月おぼろ嫁ぎし夜の空だった

米国軍人　弟ディックへ

便り来ず想ふことはるかなり戦線西南太平洋

深く息する女は女の心持ちで夏草のしげり

当時の捕虜　本田龍峰画伯よりキャソルロック山の日本画を贈らる

朝晴れ雪に深き想ひありキャソルロック山

230

Tenth Wedding Anniversary (July 3, 1944)

TSUKI OBORO TOTSUGISHI YORU NO SORA DATTA

Misty moon
as it was
on my wedding night

To Brother Dick, US soldier

TAYORI KOZU OMOU KOTO HARUKA-NARI SENSEN SEINAN TAIHEIYO

No letters
thoughts wandering
to distant South Pacific war zone

FUKAKU IKISURU ONNA WA ONNA NO KOKORO-MOCHI DE
NATSUKUSA NO SHIGERI

Breathing deeply
woman with woman's feeling
dense summer grass

To Artist Ryuho Honda

ASABARE YUKI NI FUKAKI OMOI ARI CASTLE ROCK MOUNTAIN

Clear morning evokes
deep feeling for snow
on Castle Rock Mountain

監禁者、断食する

何も見ていない心の日がつづき高原夏たけなわ

午後の陽ざし松葉ぼたんことし一重咲き

昆虫かずある夕べ吾子いよいよ成長したり

Stockade prisoners on hunger strike

NANI MO MITE INAI KOKORO NO HI GA TSUZUKI KOGEN NATSU
TAKENAWA

My heart perceives nothing
day to day
summer at its peak in highland

GOGO NO HIZASHI MATSUBABOTAN KOTOSHI HITOE-ZAKI

Afternoon sun shining
this year's moss-rose*
reverted to single petal

KONCHU KAZU ARU YUBE AKO IYO-IYO SEICHO SHITARI

Myriad insects
in the evening
my children are growing

* Moss-rose reverts to single petal after a time, thus showing years spent in
camp.

ヴァレー吟社　惜別句会　一九四四年

秋咲くものにつぼみあり今日ひとに便り書く

平井十九二

ツールレイク隔離センターにて

風吹く日雨降る日やがて来ん高原の冬

わづかのローン刈られてあり日本字の表札ある家

或は流線型のポーチなど五月雨に黒き家々

234

Valley Ginsha Farewell Haiku Meeting 1944

AKI SAKU MONO NI TSUBOMI ARI KYO HITO NI TAYORI KAKU

Buds on autumn flowering plants
today I am writing to someone

Hirai, Tokuji

KAZE FUKU HI AME FURU HI YAGATE KON KOGEN NO FUYU

Windy days, rainy days
soon winter will return
on the high plateau

WAZUKA NO LOWN KARARETE ARI NIHONJI NO HYOSATSU ARU IE

Small lawn mowed
Japanese name plate
on this house

ARU WA RYUSEN-GATA NO POOCHI NADO SAMIDARE NI KUROKI IE-IE

Some porches are streamlined★
early summer rain
on black houses (barracks)

★ Each detainee had to build his own porch to protect the entrance from the elements.

日盛り山裾小さく行く汽車の遅く

門へ抜き捨てがたし韮の花今たけなわ

蜻蛉追ふ子らに藺草木枯れたひろっぱ

シャスター山見える所まで歩き雪残る頂き

HIZAKARI YAMAZUSO CHIISAKU YUKU KISHA NO OSOKU

Midday sun on foothills
train moving slowly
and becoming smaller

KADO E NUKISUTE GATASHI NIRA NO HANA IMA TAKENAWA

Difficult to uproot
and discard outside
nira★ flower at its peak now

TOMBO OU KORA NI IGUSA KOGARETA HIROPPA

For children chasing dragonfly
withered spacious
tule reed field

SHASTA-YAMA MIERU TOKORO MADE ARUKI YUKI NOKORU ITADAKI

Walked to
where Mount Shasta is visible
snow remaining on peak

★ Chinese chives

此の夏高原に花植ゑこの国に長くいたり

一九四五年八月十六日
日本降伏の報のあとに書く

岩山に夏の月見てわたし等敵国にいる

明けくるにひまありすべてを思ひ

一九四五年八月二十六日

尾澤氏への手紙
「只今の感情、何とも表現できず」

宵月落ち寝やらぬ人のささやき

238

Written after Japan's surrender, August 16, 1945

KONO NATSU KOGEN NI HANA UE KONO KUNI NI NAGAKU ITARI

This summer planted flowers on plateau
stayed a long time
in this country

IWAYAMA★ NI NATSU NO TSUKI MITE WATASHIRA TEKIKOKU NI IRU

Looking at summer moon
on Castle Rock
we are living in alien (enemy) land

Letter to Ozawa, August 26, 1945
There is no way to express our feelings at present

AKEKURU NI HIMA ARI SUBETE O OMOI

Day in and day out
time on our hands
thinking of many things

YOITSUKI OCHI NEYARANU HITO NO SASAYAKI

Early moon has set
people unable to sleep
whispering

★ refers to Castle Rock

松田碧沙明

ツールレイク隔離センターにて

ぼつねん日なたに黒繩二三疋まふを見てゐる

人形首がとれたまま机におかれ或る夜

収容所の墓地にて

心霊碑に対ひてある想ひ此の草冷え

日本国天皇の降伏宣言を聞きつつ

しかと聴く東京（ニッポン）よりの声膝正しく聞く

240

Matsuda, Hekisamei

BOTSUNEN HINATA NI KUROBAE NISANBIKI MAU O MITE IRU

All alone in the sun
watching two or three
black flies dancing

NINGYO KUBI GA TORETA MAMA TSUKUE NI OKARE ARU YO

Doll without a head
lying on desk top
one evening

At the camp cemetery (1)

SHINREIHI NI MUKAITE ARU OMOI KONO KUSA HIE

Facing spiritual monument
thoughtfully
here, grass is cooling

SHIKA TO KIKU NIPPON YORI NO KOE HIZA TADASHIKU KIKU

Listening intently to voice
from Japan★
knees formally set

★ Japanese Emperor's surrender proclamation

こぼれ種芽ぶき何花か小さな葉をもち

ただ青く庭草のび巌山よりの風にゆれ

国戦ひて三年の夏を収容所にごぼうのび

わたしら黙したまま窓の空がからっぽで

KOBORE DANE MEBUKI NANIBANA KA CHISANA HA O MOCHI

Spilled seeds
sprouting tiny leaves
of unknown flowers

TADA AOKU NIWAKUSA NOBI IWAYAMA YORI NO KAZE NI YURE

Merely green grass
swaying in garden
wind from Castle Rock

KUNI TATAKAITE SANNEN NO NATSU O SHUYOJO NI GOBO NOBI

Nation at war three years
gobo* is growing
in concentration camp

WATASHI RA MOKUSHITA MAMA MADO NO SORA GA KAROPPO DE

We are silent
above the window
empty sky

* Burdock

松下翠香

ツールレイク隔離センターにて

貝殻に在りし世の遠くほろ〳〵崖くづれ

生くる寂しさとあり繭は花をこぼす

コスモス咲いて戦あるやうなないやうな

働けば身につきまとふ疲れ繭草枯れ敷くに寝て

244

Matsushita, Suiko

KAIGARA NI ARISHI YO NO TOOKU HOROHORO GAKE KUZURE

Oh shells—
the cliff, your bygone world
is slowly crumbling

IKURU SABISHISA TO ARI I WA HANA O KOBOSU

Facing a lonely existence
Tule reeds
shed flowers

KOSMOS SAITE TATAKAI ARUYO-NA NAIYO-NA

Cosmos in bloom
as if no war
were taking place

HATARAKEBA MINI TSUKIMATOU TSUKARE IGUSA KARE SHIKU NI NETE

Lying on dead tule reed
weariness shadows me
as I work

山時雨ひそひそ鉄柵濡らし降る

夜明ければ現実がある鉄柵の烏麦

紅芙蓉そんなもの永く忘れた

雛罌粟夕べ妻ようすものの肌匂はせ

YAMA SHIGURE HISOHISO TESSAKU NURASHI FURU

Rain shower from mountain
quietly soaking
barbed wire fence

YO AKEREBA GENZITSU GA ARU TESSAKU NO KARASUMUGI

When day breaks
reality is there
as the oats by the barbed wire fence

BENI-FUYO SONNA MONO NAGAKU WASURETA

Red *Fuyo*★
for a long time
I had forgotten such a thing

HINA-KESHI YUBE TSUMA YO USUMONO NO HADA NIOWASE

Miniature poppy
thinly clad wife
exuding fragrance—evening

★ Rose mallow

掘ればいくつも貝殻と暮れるまゝに在る

森本弥山

ツールレイク隔離センターにて

涼みがてら柵の広場にでる丸い月があり

夏山岩の上の十字架あはれインディアンの昔

天地一体麦の穂青く峯々そびゆ

HOREBA IKUTSUMO KAIGARA TO KURERUMAMA NI ARU

As I dig
many shells and I
are enveloped by dusk

Morimoto, Misen

SUZUMI GATERA SAKU NO HIROBA NI DERU MARUI TSUKI GA ARI

Strolled to cool off
into large fenced area
under the round moon

NATSU-YAMA IWA NO UENO JYUJIKA AWARE INDIAN NO MUKASHI

Summer mountain
cross on Castle Rock
pitiful last days of Indians

TENCHI ITTAI MUGINO HO AOKU MINE-MINE SOBIYU

Heaven and earth are one
wheat ears are green
soaring mountain peaks

岡本百一世

ツールレイク隔離センターにて　同胞数名検挙さる

黙ってしまった一夜いくさ話のあと炉べ

ジープ静かにはしる炉にもゆる火のあかき夜

冬夜我が肩を叩く男の色白く

嵯峨小紅子

砂塵地より吹くある日机に真向ひて座り

250

Okamoto, Hyakuissei
*Several brethren arrested after martial law was declared
at Tule Lake in November 1943*

DAMATTE SHIMATTA ICHIYA IKUSABANASHI NO ATO ROBE

Silence fell one evening
after talk of war
around fireside

JEEP SHIZUKA NI HASHIRU RONI MOYURU HINO AKAKI YORU

Jeep patrolling slowly
stove is glowing
at night

FUYUYO WAGA KATA O TATAKU OTOKO NO IRO SHIROKU

Winter night
pale faced man
taps my shoulder

Saga, Shokoshi

SHAJIN CHIYORI FUKU ARUHI TSUKUE NI MAMUKAITE SUWARI

Dust storm rising from the ground
one day I sit
facing the desk

こんなにも蒼い空鷗がゐる砂丘をのぼる

原いっぱいの風地に枯葉秋来る

不満耐えくらす萎れし花瓶の花を捨てる

喉に繃帯した少女に無風春の夜

KONNA NIMO AOI SORA KAMOME GA IRU SAKYU O NOBORU

Such a blue sky
climbing sandy hill
where seagulls are

HARA IPPAI NO KAZE CHINI KAREBA AKI KURU

Wind blows on the plain
withered leaves on ground
autumn comes

FUMAN TAE KURASHU SHIORESHI KABIN NO HANA O SUTERU

Enduring discontent
discard wilted flower
from vase

NODO NI HOOTAI SHITA SHOJO NI MUFUU HARU NO YO

For little girl
with bandage on her throat
windless spring evening

藺草細い影あり鉄柵に夕日赤い

暑さ乾いた大地に芥子の花ポタリと散る紅い

日暮れ黙って砂をふみ来て鉄柵にむかひ

相良生

ツールレイク隔離センターにて

棚に花筒あり花のない花筒

254

IGUSA HOSOI KAGE ARI TESSAKU NI YUHI AKAI

Thin shadow of tule reed
blazing sunset
on barbed wire fence

ATSUSA KAWAITA DAICHI NI KESHI NO HANA POTARI TO CHIRU AKAI

On parched soil
red poppy flower
fell audibly

HIGURE DAMATTE SUNA O FUMIKITE TESSAKU NI MUKAI

At dusk silently walked on sand
step by step
toward the barbed wire fence

Sagara, Sei

TANA NI HANATSUTSU ARI HANANO NAI HANATSUTSU

Flower vase
on shelf
no flower in vase

255

夏宵日本の歌が可愛い子の群れ

日盛り蜻蛉追う児らの歯が白い

子の花が先に咲いた快い夏の朝風

ふと目覚めて営所の喇叭を聞く月明り

NATSUYOI NIPPON NO UTA GA KAWAII KO NO MURE

Summer evening
group of cute children
singing Japanese song

HIZAKARI TOMBO OU KORA NO HA GA SHIROI

At midday
children chasing dragonflies
their teeth are white

KONO HANAGA SAKINI SAITA KOKOROYOI NATSU NO ASAKAZE

Children's flowers
bloomed first
pleasant summer morning breeze

FUTO MEZAMETE EISHO NO RAPPA O KIKU TSUKI AKARI

Suddenly awakened
listening to bugle from guard house
moonlight

虫鳴かぬ隔離所窓の月一人

ベッドにカード並べて見る一人居に広い部屋

鈴木湘南

ツールレイク隔離センターにて　一九四三年九月—一九四五年

藺草たけ風鳴る日を重ねてゐる

人ら来て湖に棲む風に耐えて咲く燕子花

MUSHI NAKANU KAKURISHO MADO NO TSUKI HITORI

No sound of insects
segregation center
moonlit window—alone

BEDDO NI KAADO NARABETE MIRU HITORI I NI HIROI HEYA

Arranging playing cards on bed
room too large
for one occupant

Suzuki, Shonan
At Tule Lake Segregation Center 1943–1945

IGUSA TAKE KAZE NARUHI O KASANETE IRU

Tule grass full-grown
wind gusting
day after day

HITORA KITE MIZUUMI NI SUMU KAZE NI TAETE SAKU KAKITSUBATA

People forced to live at lake
iris blooming
despite the wind

月影し収容所に今年も雁の声を聞く

シャスターそのままに高く野菊晴れたり

地上草枯れつくし戦車に軋しる風

冬の湖に棲む鳥のありて鉄柵とても広い

TSUKI KAGESHI SHUYOSHO NI KONNEN MO GAN NO KOE O KIKU

Moon shadows on internment camp
I hear the cries of geese
again this year

SHASTA SONOMAMA NI TAKAKU NOGIKU HARETARI

Skies cleared
Mount Shasta towering
wild camomile

CHIJO KUSAKARE TSUKUSHI SENSHA NI KISHIRU KAZE

Withered grass on ground
army tank creaking
in the wind

FUYU NO MIZUUMI NI SUMU TORI NO ARITE TETSUSAKU TOTEMO HIROI

Birds on winter lake
barbed wire fence
covers broad expanse

武田仙坊

ツールレイク隔離センターにて

静かな夜である月はかたむく巌山の影

秋陽背に住みなれし町のはなし

暮しに暇多く大人も釣る蜻蛉黒いバラック

一本の菜の花もよし庭に花なき此地

262

Takeda, Senbo

SHIZUKANA YO DE ARU TSUKI WA KATAMUKU IWAYAMA NO KAGE

A quiet night
the moon is setting
behind Castle Rock Mountain

AKIHI SE NI SUMINARESHI MACHI NO HANASHI

Autumn sun on my back
reminiscing
about familiar hometown

KURASHI NI HIMA OOKU OTONA MO TSURU TOMBO KUROI BARRAKU

Much idle time—even adults
angling for dragonflies
black barracks

IPPON NO NA-NO HANA MO YOSHI NIWA NI HANA NAKI KONOCHI

Even single mustard flower is pleasing
there are no flowers
in this place

憐れ胡蝶花たはむるに風強し

ツールレイク隔離センターにて

病葉ちるおとの朝の日に疲れをおぼゆ

夏の月代に佇ち明日も明後日も病む

庭芝青し日盛り鴨とぶ影

264

AWARE KOCHO HANA NI TAWAMURU NI KAZE TSUYOSHI

Poor butterfly fluttering
among the flowers
wind is too strong

Tateshina, Byoso

WAKURABA CHIRU OTO NO ASA NO HI NI TSUKARE O OBOYU

Morning sun
the sound of falling diseased leaves
makes me feel tired

NATSU NO TSUKISHIRO NI TACHI ASU MO ASSATE MO YAMU

Lingering in the summer moonlight
I will be ill
tomorrow and the day after

NIWASHIBA AOSHI HIZAKARI KAMO TOBU KAGE

The lawn is green
in the heat of day
shadow of flying duck

上丸子雫

夏朝鴨を呼ぶ草は穂にいでし

今朝からのちぐはぐな心に日傘さして出る

高い山低い山晴れて葱坊主花咲き

寂寥山の雲草にバッタ飛び立ち

Uyemaruko, Shizuku

NATSU ASA KAMO O YOBU KUSA WA HO NI IDESHI

Summer morning
calling wild ducks
shoots appearing on grass

KESA KARA NO CHIGUHAGUNA KOKORO NI HIGASA SASHITE DERU

Uneasy feeling
since this morning
leaving with a parasol

TAKAI YAMA HIKUI YAMA HARETE NEGIBOZU HANA SAKI

High and low mountains
clear day
onion pods blooming

SEKIRYO YAMANO KUMO KUSA NI BATTA TOBI TACHI

Loneliness
clouds on mountain
grasshopper jumped from grass

軒低い家に子供泣き葦の花

砂風吹きこむ室の額の位置をかへる

生くる身に解せぬ事多く夏星光る

ある日は白々しい心に見る牛蒡の花むらさき

268

NOKI HIKUI IE NI KODOMO NAKI ASHI NO HANA

In the house with low eaves
a child cries
reed flowers

SUNAKAZE FUKIKOMU HEYA NO GAKU NO ICHI O KAERU

Changing position of picture
sand blows
into the room

IKURU MI NI GESENU KOTO OOKU NATSU-HOSHI HIKARU

For the living
many incomprehensible incidents
summer stars shine

ARUHI WA SHIRAJIRASHII KOKORO NI MIRU GOBO NO HANA MURASAKI

On certain days
heart is full of hypocrisy
flowers of *gobo** are purple

* Burdock

無心にトンボ追ふ少年の靴のやぶれさみし

悼古賀司令長官

鴨鳴かぬ日はさみし鳴けばさみし五月山の日

和田白露

若草が赤くちじれた砂原が広い砂風

童女ゆがんだ靴が体列を走る夏の朝

MUSHIN NI TOMBO OU SHONEN NO KUTSU NO YABURE SAMISHI

Innocently chasing dragonflies
child with worn shoes
what sadness!

Mourn Death of Japanese Admiral Koga

KAMO NAKANU HI WA SAMISHI NAKEBA SAMISHI GOGATSU
YAMANO NO HI

Whether the gulls cry or not
I am lonely
mountain sun in May

Wada, Hakuro

WAKAKUSA GA AKAKU CHIZIRETA SUNABARA GA HIROI SUNAKAZE

Young grass red and shriveled
wide sandy flat
and gritty wind

DOJO YUGANDA KUTSU GA TAIRETSU O HASHIRU NATSU NO ASA

Young girl with worn out shoes
running in formation
summer morning

真夏の月があをじろい高原の街だ

鷗の腹に日本と朱書きして放す高原の初夏

かわず鳴く音も柵外にして我等の暮らし

MANATSU NO TSUKI GA AOJIROI KOGEN NO MACHI DA

Midsummer moon
pale blue
a gloomy community on the plain

KAMOME NO HARA NI NIPPON TO SHUGAKI–SHITE HANASU KOGEN
NO SHOKA

Released seagull
after writing NIPPON in red on its belly
summer morning in highlands

KAWAZU NAKU OTO MO SAKUGAI NI SHITE WARERA NO KURASHI

Even the croaking of frogs
comes from outside the barbed wire fence
this is our life

一九四四年五月二十四日岡本青年、ツールレイクにて狙撃され、死亡

岡本青年の死を悼む

平井十九二

たゞ夏の青い空あり男らもの云わず

高原やうやく夏めき禿山のうねりに雲の影

岡本百一世

たんぽぽの穂長（た）けたるに怨むこの時なんの時

274

Shooting Death of Okamoto

Soichi James Okamoto, a construction worker, was asking permission to pass through the Tule Lake Camp gate when he was fatally shot, on May 24, 1944. The sentry who fired the fatal bullet was later acquitted after being fined $1.00 for the "unauthorized use of government property." The next 10 haiku are about Okamoto's death.

Hirai, Tokuji

TADA NATSU NO AOI SORA ARI OTOKORA MONO IWAZU

Only the blue summer sky
the men
are silent

KOGEN YOYAKU NATSUMEKI HAGEYAMA NO UNERI NI KUMO NO KAGE

Plateau finally summery
clouds cast meandering shadows
on bare hills

Okamoto, Hyakuissei

TAMPOPO NO HO TAKETARUNI URAMU KONO TOKI NANNO TOKI

Dandelion has bloomed
a moment of bitterness—
of what consequence?

275

岡本青年葬儀

平井十九二

曇る空を雁一聯音なく人数千

鈴木湘南

草原立木なく西日に飛んでゆき燕

上丸子雫

同胞またたほれ地のからす麦

276

Funeral of Okamoto

Hirai, Tokuji

KUMORU SORA O GAN ICHIREN OTO NAKU HITO SUSEN

Cloudy sky
row of wild geese
and soundless multitude

Suzuki, Shonan

KUSAHARA TACHIKI NAKU NISHIBI NI TONDE YUKI TSUBAME

Treeless plain
swallows fly
toward setting sun

Uyemaruko, Shizuku

HARA KARA MATA TAORE CHI NO KARASUMUGI

Grieving within
another victim
oats on the ground

相良生

同胞の死を悼しむや切雨蕭条

松下翠香

柩を送って刈り草乾く砂の風ばかり

松田一恵

或日は泣いてもみたしこんな日々曇天つづく

松田碧沙明

柩車見送るはらからに五月末日の雨降り

278

Sagara, Sei

DOHO NO SHI O ITAMUYA SETSU AME-SHOJYO

Death of brethren
mourning intensely
rain falling drearily

Matsushita, Suiko

HITSUGI O OKUTTE KARIKUSA KAWAKU SUNA NO KAZE BAKARI

Send off casket
clippings drying, and
only the sandy wind

Matsuda, Kazue

ARUHI WA NAITE MO MITASHI KONNA HIBI DONTEN TSUZUKU

Some days I feel like crying
these days are
continuously cloudy

Matsuda, Hekisamei

KYUSHA MIOKURU HARAKARANI GOGATSU MATSUJITSU NO AMEFURI

Sending off comrade's hearse
last day of May
rain falling

A funeral at Tule Lake

Epilogue

Through the mist of the surging seas
has emerged a beacon to help us
recall our past and guide us on
our course
—ANONYMOUS

About the Compiler

Katsuichi Yamane and Shika Furukawa Yamane, my parents, were Issei immigrants from Hiroshima Prefecture. They lived near Hilo, Hawaii, in order to be close to their relatives' place of work, Halakau Plantation.

I was born not far from Hilo, in Ninole, on January 3, 1917. I attended Ninole primary school and the Japanese Language School until 1924. When my family returned to Hiroshima, they enrolled me in the Danbara Elementary School.

When I was in my mid-teens, my parents decided I should be receiving an American education and arrangements were made for me to move to Fresno, California. I stayed with friends of the family, Mr. and Mrs. Theodore M. Stuart, who immediately enrolled me in Roosevelt High School, and raised me as their own daughter.

Mr. Stuart, an attorney who also represented the Bank of Italy and the Santa Fe Railway Company, strongly influenced my appreciation of justice and fair play, especially at a time when it was being severely taxed by the subtle discriminatory practices perpetrated against relatives and friends who, because of their Oriental lineage, were forced to live "across the tracks."

Upon graduation from high school, I married Shigeru Matsuda, a charter member of the Valley Ginsha Haiku Kai and subsequently became a member of the Kaiko (free style)

283

School of Haiku. It was at that time that I met Neiji Ozawa, the leader of the Valley Ginsha Haiku Kai, and the Rev. Chisan Taira, who later became our *Baishaku-Nin* (marriage go-betweens).

In 1939, I took my children, Kenji and Reiko, for an extended visit to see my parents in Hiroshima City. My stay in Japan gave me the opportunity to complete my classical education, including the finer points of haiku, and to travel extensively with my mother, enhancing my appreciation of Japanese culture.

Returning to America prior to the outbreak of World War II, I was appalled to learn that the family bank accounts, totaling over $27,000, had been frozen by the US government under the Enemy Alien Act. Shortly thereafter, as a result of the signing of Executive Order 9066 by President Franklin Delano Roosevelt, my family and I were forced to abandon our home and all of our possessions, including the Matsuda Book Store which we owned, and were immediately relocated to the Fresno Assembly Center. Several months later, we were transferred to the Jerome Concentration Camp in the swampland of Arkansas and, in the fall of 1943, to the Tule Lake Segregation Center in Northern California. Tule Lake was our "home" until March 1946 when my children and I were expatriated to Japan.

By that time, my mother-in-law had died at Tule Lake, and my father-in-law, my husband, and my brother Tokio had already been sent to Japan. When we arrived in Hiroshima, the atomic bomb had already been dropped. My father and mother were victims of the explosion, their home had been demolished. I also found out that my husband had remarried.

The war-devastated economy had resulted in a thriving black market, and people had been reduced to bartering their few remaining possessions to survive. In order to support myself and my children, I had to work three jobs, concurrently, because I was being paid in devalued yen, as other American expatriates were, instead of dollars.

My present husband and I were married in 1953. From 1961 until I retired in 1980, I was employed by CTB/McGraw-Hill, a publishing firm in Monterey, California, as Systems and Program Coordinator.

In 1981, I testified before the (Congressional) Commission on Wartime Relocation and Internment of Civilians (CWRIC) on the socio-psychological impact of the internment, as well as continuing my active support of Redress Legislation to its successful conclusion. I have also continued to contribute regularly to the *Kaiko Haiku Journal* of Tokyo, Japan.

In 1984, I was instrumental in erecting and dedicating California Registered Historical Landmark No. 934, at the location of the former Salinas Assembly Center; and, in 1987, I published *Ino Hana: Poetic Reflections of Tule Lake Internment—1944*, the few remaining haiku of the many I had written during my internment. (They are also currently being included in several American college and high school textbooks.)

Of the hundreds of English and Japanese haiku submitted at the US-Japan Conference on Haiku Poetry, sponsored by the Museum of Haiku Literature and Japan Air Lines, held in San Francisco in 1987, I was one of the few who received Honorable Mention for my submission.

In the spring of 1995, the Japanese edition of this anthology was published in Kyoto and was acclaimed by the Japanese media for filling a gap in the readers' knowledge of the Japanese-American internment and in the war-time literary activities of the Kaiko Haiku poets in North America.

My internment experiences have also been published in *Rikka*, a Canadian cross-cultural publication, in an anthology of Chinese-American and Japanese-American literature, and in *Amerasia*, the journal of the Asian-American Studies Center at the University of California at Los Angeles.

On the 50th anniversary of the Pearl Harbor attack, my brother Tokio Yamane, who resides in Japan, and I were interviewed by NHK, the Japanese Broadcast Corporation, about the little-known episode of the post-war expatriation of Japanese Americans. The program, accentuating Robert Burns' maxim that:

> *Man's inhumanity to man*
> *Makes countless thousands mourn*

was broadcast on prime time, throughout Japan, on December 4, 1991.

Acknowledgments

I am indebted to all the internee poets whose haiku I have used in this volume, and to all others who have made available to me the few remaining original haiku, illustrations or biographical data on the writers.

I thank the McGraw-Hill Foundation of New York City, and those scholars who have been of invaluable assistance to me, because without their resource material, encouragement, helpful suggestions, erudite comments, and energetic support, this project might not have been completed. I particularly want to thank the following:

Dr Kazuo Sato of Waseda University, Tokyo, President of the International Division of the Haiku Museum of Japan; Dr Makoto Ueda, Chairman of the Asian Studies Department and Professor of Japanese and Comparative Literature, Stanford University, Palo Alto; Dr Peter Suzuki of the University of Nebraska, Omaha; Mr Mayumi Nakatsuka, son of the late Ippekiro Nakatsuka, and founder of the Kaiko Free-Style (one-line) School of Haiku.

And I respectfully thank Mr Rashi Ozaki, formerly of the Japanese Foreign Office, and author of *A Study of Nakatsuka, Ippekiro*; Mr Isshi Fukushima, author of *Seeking The Origin and Flow of Kaiko*; Mr Masato Ozawa, author of *Byoshu* and son of the late Neiji Ozawa, founder and leader of the North America School of Kaiko Haiku; Professor Iwao Yamamoto of Ritsumeikan University; and Mr Kunihito Sawada of Korosha, Kyoto, Japan, for their efforts in making the Japanese edition conceivable.

I remain forever grateful to all others who have made possible my dream of honoring the Kaiko haiku writers of the war period become a reality after half a century.

With profound appreciation

Violet Kazue de Cristoforo

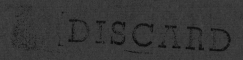